Southern Living®
Home Cooking
favorites

© 2011 by Time Home Entertainment Inc.
135 West 50th Street, New York, NY 10020

ISBN-10: 0-8487-3954-X
ISBN-13: 978-0-8487-3954-6

Printed in the United States of America
Second Printing 2013

Oxmoor House

VP, Publishing Director: Jim Childs
Editorial Director: Susan Payne Dobbs
Brand Manager: Daniel Fagan
Senior Editor: Rebecca Brennan
Managing Editor: Laurie S. Herr

Home Cooking Favorites

Editors: Julie Gunter, Susan Hernandez Ray
Project Editor: Holly D. Smith
Designer: Melissa Clark
Assistant Designer: Allison L. Sperando
Director, Test Kitchens: Elizabeth Tyler Austin
Assistant Director, Test Kitchens: Julie Christopher
Test Kitchens Professionals: Wendy Ball, Allison E. Cox, Victoria E. Cox, Margaret Monroe Dickey, Alyson Moreland Haynes, Callie Nash, Kathleen Royal Phillips, Catherine Crowell Steele, Leah Van Deren
Photography Director: Jim Bathie
Senior Photo Stylist: Kay E. Clarke
Associate Photo Stylist: Katherine Eckert Coyne
Assistant Photo Stylist: Mary Louise Menendez
Senior Production Manager: Greg A. Amason

Contributors:

Compositor: Carol Damsky
Copy Editor: Donna Baldone
Food Stylists: Ana Price Kelly, Debby Maugans
Photographers: Tina Cornett, Will Dickey, Beau Gustafson, Lee Harrelson, Beth Dreiling Hontzas, Art Meripol, Mark Sandlin, Karim Shamsi-Basha, Amy Jo Young
Photo Stylists: Mindi Shapiro Levine, Leslie Simpson
Proofreader: Lauren Brooks
Indexer: Nanette Cardon
Intern: Caitlin Watzke

Southern Living

Executive Editor: Rachel Hardage
Food Director: Shannon Sliter Satterwhite
Senior Food Writer: Donna Florio
Senior Food Editors: Shirley Harrington, Mary Allen Perry
Recipe Editor: JoAnn Weatherly
Copy Editor: Ashley Leath
Assistant Recipe Editor: Ashley Arthur
Test Kitchen Director: Rebecca Kracke Gordon
Test Kitchen Specialists/Food Styling: Marian Cooper Cairns, Vanessa McNeil Rocchio
Test Kitchens Professionals: Norman King, Pam Lolley, Angela Sellers
Senior Photographers: Ralph Anderson, Jennifer Davick
Senior Photo Stylist: Buffy Hargett
Assistant Photo Stylist: Amy Burke
Studio Assistant: Caroline Murphy
Editorial Assistant: Pat York
Photo Research Coordinator: Ginny P. Allen
Production Coordinator: Paula Dennis

To order additional publications, call 1-800-765-6400 or 1-800-491-0551.
To search, savor, and share thousands of recipes, visit **myrecipes.com**

Cover: Four-Cheese Macaroni, page 143
Back cover: (from top left) Chicken Pot Pie, page 35; Patriotic Cupcakes, page 346; Triple-Decker Strawberry Cake, page 288; Corn Pudding, page 184

Southern Living

Home Cooking
favorites

Oxmoor
House®

contents

Three-Cheese Pasta Bake,
page 10

Welcome

Take a delicious walk with us down memory lane and follow your heart home as we reminisce about some of the South's most beloved recipes. Explore the kinds of flavorful dishes that are shared at supper clubs, swapped at garden groups, and passed down from grandmother to granddaughter. Generations of home cooks have given us some of their best recipes, full of warm memories of family and friends. After testing and sampling thousands of these recipes over the years, we've handpicked this cherished collection—a tough job, I assure you.

In this book, you'll find exceptional recipes for busy weeknights, casual gatherings, and just pure enjoyment. Among them is one of my all-time favorites, **Three-Cheese Pasta Bake** (page 10)—a melt-in-your-mouth taste experience that will change the way you think about mac and cheese. Don't miss **Uptown Banana Pudding Cheesecake** (page 64) that combines two classic desserts in one. No true Southerner can resist this creamy banana sensation baked in a vanilla-wafer crust. If weeknight comfort is what you crave, then be sure to add **Quick-and-Easy King Ranch Chicken Casserole** (page 133) to your recipe files: soft, warm, cheesy layers of chicken and tortilla chips with a subtle hint of green chile.

Of course, all dishes must undergo strict scrutiny among our Food staff before they can truly be called *Southern Living* recipes. Daily tastings offer a wealth of food knowledge that we've sprinkled throughout these pages, passing along some of our best tips and techniques. For example, discover a healthy secret to making **Kentucky Burgoo** (page 19). And, learn the best way to prepare corn for **Tee's Corn Pudding** (page 183).

Best of all, everything is easy. No more guesswork on what to serve for supper or at your next gathering. Just pick what you like and go with it. You are sure to find some favorites that you can someday pass down to your loved ones.

Enjoy!

Shannon

Shannon Sliter Satterwhite
Southern Living Food Director

Gonzales Meat Loaf and Home-Cooked
Pole Beans, page 14

blue-ribbon classics

Three-Cheese Pasta Bake

prep: 20 min. • cook: 7 min. • bake: 15 min.

Mac and cheese, the quintessential comfort food, gets a great update with penne pasta and a trio of cheeses.

1 (8-ounce) package penne pasta
2 tablespoons butter
2 tablespoons all-purpose flour
1½ cups milk
½ cup half-and-half
1 cup (4 ounces) shredded white Cheddar cheese

¼ cup grated Parmesan cheese
2 cups (8 ounces) shredded Gruyère cheese, divided
1 teaspoon salt
¼ teaspoon pepper
Pinch of ground nutmeg

1. Preheat oven to 350°. Prepare pasta according to package directions.
2. Meanwhile, melt butter in a saucepan over medium heat. Whisk in flour until smooth; cook, whisking constantly, 1 minute. Gradually whisk in milk and half-and-half; cook, whisking constantly, 3 to 5 minutes or until thickened. Stir in Cheddar cheese, Parmesan cheese, 1 cup Gruyère cheese, and next 3 ingredients until smooth.
3. Stir together pasta and cheese mixture; pour into a lightly greased 11- x 7-inch baking dish. Top with remaining 1 cup Gruyère cheese.
4. Bake, uncovered, at 350° for 15 minutes or until golden and bubbly. **Yield:** 4 servings.

Note: To make ahead, proceed with recipe as directed, but don't top with remaining 1 cup Gruyère cheese. Cover and chill up to 8 hours. Let stand at room temperature 30 minutes. Bake at 350° for 20 to 25 minutes or until bubbly. Increase oven temperature to 400°. Top with remaining Gruyère; bake 10 more minutes or until golden.

Everyone will **love** this and want the recipe! It's velvety, **creamy** texture is like a pasta you would get at a restaurant.

Barbecue Deviled Eggs

prep: 30 min. • cook: 6 min. • stand: 15 min.

Chopped barbecued pork is the filling's secret ingredient in this old-fashioned Southern favorite. If you want to omit the chopped pork, add a drop of liquid smoke to provide a barbecue-like flavor.

12	large eggs		⅛	teaspoon hot sauce
¼	cup mayonnaise		⅓	cup finely chopped barbecued pork
1	tablespoon Dijon mustard			(without sauce)
¼	teaspoon salt			Garnishes: paprika, chopped dill pickle
½	teaspoon pepper			

make ahead • portable

1. Place eggs in a single layer in a large saucepan; add water to a depth of 3 inches. Bring to a boil; cover, remove from heat, and let stand 15 minutes.

2. Drain and fill pan with cold water and ice. Tap each egg firmly on counter until cracks form all over shell. Peel under cold running water.

3. Cut eggs in half lengthwise, and carefully remove yolks. Mash yolks with mayonnaise. Stir in mustard and next 3 ingredients; blend well. Gently stir in pork.

4. Spoon yolk mixture into egg white halves.

5. Chill until ready to serve. Garnish, if desired. **Yield:** 12 servings.

Wow your family and friends by serving this scrumptious **Southern** favorite at your next Fourth of July party or backyard cookout.

Gonzales Meat Loaf

prep: 15 min. • bake: 1 hr. • stand: 10 min.

Cilantro, brown sugar, and a heavy shake of hot sauce deliver big flavor to this meat loaf. Leftovers make a great sandwich.

make ahead • portable

2 pounds ground sirloin
3 large eggs, lightly beaten
1 cup fine, dry breadcrumbs
4 garlic cloves, minced
1 medium-size red onion, chopped
2 plum tomatoes, seeded and chopped
1½ cups (6 ounces) shredded Monterey Jack cheese
¼ to ½ cup firmly packed brown sugar
½ cup chopped fresh cilantro
¼ cup Worcestershire sauce
2 tablespoons hot sauce
2 teaspoons salt
1 teaspoon pepper

1. Preheat oven to 350°. Combine all ingredients. Shape into a free-form 9- x 5-inch loaf, and place on a lightly greased rack in a broiler pan.
2. Bake at 350° for 45 minutes; increase oven temperature to 425°, and bake 15 to 25 more minutes or until done. Let meat loaf stand 10 minutes before serving. **Yield:** 6 to 8 servings.

Yummy! This meat loaf is definitely delicious! Lining the pan with **aluminum foil** makes clean up a breeze!

Home-Cooked Pole Beans

prep: 26 min. • cook: 19 min.

2 pounds fresh pole beans
3 bacon slices
1 teaspoon salt
½ teaspoon pepper
¼ teaspoon sugar

1. Wash beans; trim stem ends. Cut beans into 1½-inch pieces, and set aside.
2. Cook bacon in a large saucepan until crisp; remove bacon, reserving drippings in pan. Crumble bacon, and set aside.
3. Add 1 cup water and remaining 3 ingredients to saucepan; bring to a boil over high heat. Add beans; cover, reduce heat to medium, and cook 15 minutes or to desired doneness. Sprinkle with crumbled bacon. Serve with a slotted spoon. **Yield:** 8 servings.

Buttermilk-Garlic Mashed Potatoes

prep: 10 min. • cook: 6 min.

2	tablespoons butter		½	teaspoon salt
3	garlic cloves, chopped		½	teaspoon pepper
2	cups buttermilk		1	(22-ounce) package frozen mashed potatoes
⅔	cup milk			

1. Melt butter in a Dutch oven over medium heat; add garlic, and sauté 1 minute.
2. Add buttermilk and next 3 ingredients. Cook, stirring constantly, 5 minutes or until thoroughly heated. Stir in potatoes until smooth. **Yield:** 4 servings.

Note: We tested with Ore-Ida Mashed Potatoes. There's no need to thaw them.

Beef Stroganoff

prep: 16 min. • cook: 41 min.

A universal homey entrée, this stroganoff turns out a big yield with plenty of gravy for sopping.

1	cup all-purpose flour		2	garlic cloves, minced
1½	teaspoons salt		½	cup dry sherry or dry white wine
½	teaspoon pepper		3	cups beef broth
2	pounds sirloin steak, cut into strips		2	tablespoons tomato paste
½	cup butter, melted		1	tablespoon Dijon mustard
2	tablespoons butter		1	tablespoon Worcestershire sauce
1	(8-ounce) package sliced fresh mushrooms		1	(16-ounce) container sour cream
1	small onion, chopped			Hot cooked egg noodles or mashed potatoes
				Chopped fresh parsley

1. Combine first 3 ingredients in a large zip-top plastic freezer bag; add steak. Seal bag, and shake until meat is coated.

2. Brown meat in ½ cup butter in a sauté pan or large skillet over medium-high heat. Remove meat from pan; cover and keep warm. Add 2 tablespoons butter to hot pan; sauté mushrooms, onion, and garlic until browned and tender. Remove from pan; keep warm.

3. Add sherry or wine to pan; cook over high heat, stirring to loosen particles from bottom of pan. Add beef broth and next 3 ingredients, stirring until smooth. Return meat and sautéed mushroom mixture to pan; cook over medium heat until thickened, stirring frequently. Stir in sour cream; cook just until thoroughly heated. Serve over egg noodles or mashed potatoes; sprinkle with parsley. **Yield:** 6 to 8 servings.

Kentucky Burgoo

prep: 1 hr., 50 min. • cook: 5 hr., 10 min. • chill: 8 hr.

In Kentucky, burgoo is a favorite church supper or fund-raiser dinner that's cooked by a crowd and eaten by a crowd. Traditionally, it contained mutton that was raised in the state.

1	(3- to 4-pound) cut-up whole chicken		1	cup frozen baby lima beans
1	(2-pound) beef chuck roast		1	cup frozen English peas
2	pounds pork loin chops, trimmed		3	garlic cloves, minced
5	quarts water		2	(32-ounce) containers beef broth
1	rabbit, dressed (optional)		1	(32-ounce) bottle ketchup
1	pound tomatoes		2	cups dry red wine
5	large potatoes		1	(10-ounce) bottle Worcestershire sauce
5	celery ribs		¼	cup white vinegar
4	carrots		1	tablespoon salt
2	onions		1	tablespoon pepper
2	green bell peppers		1	tablespoon dried thyme
1	small cabbage			Crackers (optional)
2	cups frozen whole kernel corn			

1. Bring first 4 ingredients and rabbit, if desired, to a boil in a 4-gallon heavy stockpot. Cover, reduce heat, and simmer 1 hour or until tender. Remove meats from stockpot, and cool. Skin, bone, and shred meats; return meats to stockpot.

2. Cover and chill soup overnight. Skim solidified fat from surface. Chop tomatoes and next 5 ingredients. Shred cabbage. Add prepared vegetables, corn, and remaining ingredients to soup; cook over low heat, stirring often, 4 hours. Serve with crackers, if desired. **Yield:** 11 quarts.

Note: Portion leftovers into individual servings in airtight containers, and freeze up to 2 months.

Test Kitchen Tip

Chilling the soup overnight allows the fat to solidify and rise to the surface, making it easier to skim.

Lemon-Garlic Roast Chicken With Sautéed Green Beans

prep: 10 min. • bake: 1 hr., 10 min. • stand: 10 min. • cook: 5 min.

After roasting the chicken, sauté some green beans in the rich pan juices.

3	tablespoons chopped fresh parsley	½	teaspoon pepper
2	tablespoons butter, softened	1	(4-pound) whole chicken
2	tablespoons olive oil	1	(12-ounce) bag fresh green beans or
2	teaspoons lemon zest	1	(16-ounce) package frozen whole
2	garlic cloves, pressed		green beans
1	teaspoon salt		

Garnishes: lemon wedges, fresh parsley sprigs

1. Preheat oven to 450°. Stir together first 7 ingredients. Starting at neck cavity, loosen skin from chicken breast and drumsticks by inserting fingers and gently pushing between skin and meat. (Do not completely detach skin.) Rub half of butter mixture under skin. Carefully replace skin.

2. Tie ends of legs together with string; tuck wing tips under. Spread remaining half of butter mixture over chicken. Place chicken, breast side up, on a lightly greased rack in a lightly greased shallow roasting pan. Bake at 450° for 30 minutes.

3. Reduce oven temperature to 350°, and bake 40 minutes or until a meat thermometer inserted into thigh registers 170°. Cover chicken loosely with aluminum foil to prevent excessive browning, if necessary. Remove chicken to a serving platter, reserving drippings in pan. Cover chicken with foil, and let stand 10 minutes before slicing.

4. Bring pan juices to a boil in a large skillet; add green beans, and cook 5 to 7 minutes or to desired tenderness. Season with salt and pepper to taste. Serve beans on platter with chicken. Garnish, if desired. **Yield:** 4 servings.

Garlic-Herb Roasted Chicken

prep: 10 min. • bake: 1 hr., 15 min. • stand: 10 min.

Add additional moistness and flavor by replacing the wire roasting rack with a colorful rack of carrots and celery ribs. Tuck in a few sprigs of fresh herbs, some unpeeled whole shallots, and apple slices.

3	garlic cloves, minced		1	teaspoon chopped fresh sage
2	teaspoons chopped fresh thyme		1	teaspoon salt
2	teaspoons chopped fresh rosemary		¾	teaspoon freshly ground pepper
2	teaspoons chopped fresh parsley		1	(4- to 5-pound) whole chicken

1. Preheat oven to 450°. Stir together first 7 ingredients.

2. If applicable, remove giblets from chicken, and reserve for another use. Rinse chicken, and pat dry. Gently loosen and lift skin from breast and drumsticks with fingers. (Do not totally detach skin.) Rub herb mixture underneath skin. Carefully replace skin. Place chicken, breast side up, on a lightly greased wire rack in a lightly greased shallow roasting pan. Tie ends of legs together with string; tuck wing tips under.

3. Bake at 450° for 30 minutes. Reduce heat to 350°, and bake 45 minutes or until a meat thermometer inserted in thigh registers 180°, covering loosely with aluminum foil to prevent excessive browning, if necessary. Let chicken stand, covered, 10 minutes before slicing.
Yield: 4 to 6 servings.

This **flavorful** main dish works well for special occasions and for weeknight **family** dinners.

The Perfect Burgers

prep: 10 min. • stand: 35 min. • grill: 16 min.

A simple, rustic burger right off the grill is every man's favorite dish.

1½   pounds ground beef (75/25 or 25% fat)
1½   teaspoons kosher salt
1½   teaspoons coarsely ground pepper
6   (1-ounce) Cheddar cheese slices

6   hamburger buns
Toppings: lettuce leaves, red onion slices, tomato slices

1. Gently combine beef, salt, and pepper. Shape into 6 (4-inch) 1-inch-thick patties. Using thumb and forefinger, lightly press middle of patties, pressing in but not completely through, creating an indentation in center of patties. Let stand at room temperature 30 minutes.
2. Preheat grill to 350° to 400° (medium-high). Grill, covered with grill lid, 6 to 7 minutes on each side or until no longer pink in center. Top each burger with 1 cheese slice, and grill, covered with grill lid, 1 to 2 minutes or until cheese is melted. Remove from grill, and let stand 5 minutes. Serve on hamburger buns with desired toppings. **Yield:** 6 burgers.

French Fries

prep: 30 min. • cook: 5 min. per batch

These russet strips are twice-fried for extra-crispy results.

4   pounds russet or Idaho potatoes, peeled
Vegetable oil

Salt to taste

1. Cut potatoes into ¼-inch-wide strips.
2. Pour vegetable oil to a depth of 4 inches in a Dutch oven, and heat to 325°. Fry potato strips, in batches, until lightly golden but not brown, 4 to 5 minutes per batch. Drain strips on paper towels.
3. Heat oil to 375°. Fry strips, in small batches, until golden brown and crisp, 1 to 2 minutes per batch. Drain on clean paper towels. Sprinkle strips with salt, and serve immediately. **Yield:** 6 servings.

Variation
Salt-and-Pepper Fries: Prepare French Fries as directed. Grind some fresh pepper over hot fries after you sprinkle them with salt.

"Nothing says summertime quite like **burgers on the grill** loaded with melted cheese, lettuce, red onion, and fresh, juicy tomato slices."

Sweet-and-Savory Burgers

prep: 15 min. • grill: 10 min. • chill: 4 hr.

Press your thumb into centers of patties, before grilling, for burgers that cook up flat, rather than domed, across the top.

¼	cup soy sauce		2	pounds ground beef
2	tablespoons light corn syrup		¼	cup chili sauce
1	tablespoon fresh lemon juice		¼	cup hot red pepper jelly
½	teaspoon ground ginger		8	hamburger buns, toasted
¼	teaspoon garlic powder		Toppings: grilled sweet onion and pineapple slices	
2	green onions, thinly sliced			

1. Stir together first 6 ingredients. Reserve 3 tablespoons mixture; cover and chill. Pour remaining soy sauce mixture into a shallow pan or baking dish.

2. Shape beef into 8 (½-inch-thick) patties; place in a single layer in soy sauce mixture in pan, turning to coat. Cover and chill 4 hours.

3. Preheat grill to 350° to 400° (medium-high) heat. Remove patties from marinade, discarding marinade. Grill patties, covered with grill lid, 5 minutes on each side or until beef is no longer pink in center, basting occasionally with reserved 3 tablespoons soy sauce mixture.

4. Stir together chili sauce and jelly. Serve burgers on buns with chili sauce mixture and desired toppings. **Yield:** 8 servings.

This **unique** burger boasts a soy-based marinade with **sweet and spicy** ingredients and is topped with grilled sweet onion and pineapple slices.

Fried Hot Dogs

prep: 5 min. • cook: 4 min.

Try these skillet-fried dogs on hamburger buns with popular burger toppings, or use hot dog buns and chop the toppings instead of slicing. Or skip the toppings, and douse the dogs with the chili featured below.

4	hot dogs		4	tomato slices
¼	cup mayonnaise		4	onion slices
¼	cup mustard		4	lettuce leaves
4	hamburger buns, toasted			

1. Cut a slit lengthwise in each hot dog, cutting to, but not through, other side. Place hot dogs, flat sides down, in a skillet, and cook over medium-high heat 2 minutes on each side or until well browned. Drain hot dogs on paper towels, if desired.

2. Stir together mayonnaise and mustard; spread on bun halves. Place 1 hot dog on bottom half of each bun. Top with tomato, onion, lettuce, and remaining bun halves. **Yield:** 4 servings.

Hot Dog Chili

prep: 10 min. • cook: 1 hr.

Serve on hot dogs along with a pile of shredded Cheddar and finely chopped onion.

2	pounds lean ground beef		1	cup ketchup
1	small onion, finely chopped		4	teaspoons Worcestershire sauce
1	teaspoon vegetable oil		1	teaspoon white vinegar
1	teaspoon salt		½	teaspoon dry mustard
4	teaspoons chili powder		¼	to ½ teaspoon pepper

1. Cook ground beef in a Dutch oven over medium-high heat, stirring until beef crumbles and is no longer pink; drain well. Wipe Dutch oven clean with a paper towel.

2. Sauté onion in hot oil in Dutch oven 5 minutes. Add salt, chili powder, and beef, and cook 3 to 5 minutes. Stir in 2¼ cups water, ketchup, and next 4 ingredients. Bring to a boil; reduce heat to low, and simmer, stirring occasionally, 45 minutes or until most of liquid evaporates. **Yield:** 5 cups.

Basic Buttermilk Cornbread

prep: 18 min. • bake: 30 min.

¼   cup butter

1½ cups buttermilk

1   large egg

2   cups self-rising cornmeal mix

1. Preheat oven to 425°. Melt butter in a 10-inch cast-iron skillet in oven 8 minutes.

2. Whisk together buttermilk and egg in a large bowl; add melted butter from skillet, whisking until blended. Whisk in cornmeal until smooth. Spoon into hot skillet.

3. Bake at 425° for 30 minutes or until golden. Cut into wedges to serve. **Yield:** 8 servings.

Ham-and-Greens Pot Pie With Cornbread Crust

prep: 15 min. • cook: 40 min. • bake: 20 min. • stand: 10 min.

4   cups chopped cooked ham
2   tablespoons vegetable oil
3   tablespoons all-purpose flour
3   cups chicken broth
1   (16-ounce) package frozen seasoning
     blend

1   (16-ounce) package frozen chopped
     collard greens
1   (16-ounce) can black-eyed peas, rinsed
     and drained
½   teaspoon dried crushed red pepper
     Cornbread Crust Batter

make ahead

1. Preheat oven to 425°.

2. Sauté ham in hot oil in a Dutch oven over medium-high heat 5 minutes or until lightly browned. Add flour, and cook, stirring constantly, 1 minute. Gradually add chicken broth, and cook, stirring constantly, 3 minutes or until broth begins to thicken.

3. Bring mixture to a boil, and add seasoning blend and collard greens; return to a boil, and cook, stirring often, 15 minutes. Stir in black-eyed peas and crushed red pepper; spoon hot mixture into a lightly greased 13- x 9-inch baking dish.

4. Pour Cornbread Crust Batter over hot filling mixture. Bake at 425° for 20 to 25 minutes or until cornbread is golden brown and set. Let stand 10 minutes before serving. **Yield:** 8 to 10 servings.

Note: To get a head start on this recipe, make it a day in advance through Step 3; cover and refrigerate. The following day, simply reheat the filling in the microwave; uncover and continue with Step 4.

Cornbread Crust Batter

prep: 10 min.

1½   cups white cornmeal mix
½   cup all-purpose flour
1   teaspoon sugar

2   large eggs, lightly beaten
1½   cups buttermilk

1. Combine first 3 ingredients; make a well in the center of mixture. Add eggs and buttermilk to cornmeal mixture, stirring just until moistened. **Yield:** makes enough batter for 1 (13- x 9-inch) crust.

Egg Salad Sandwiches

prep: 13 min.

You can also use this egg salad to make finger sandwiches on thin white bread; or smear it on crostini, and top it with fresh herbs.

make ahead • portable

6	large hard-cooked eggs	½	teaspoon Dijon mustard
2	tablespoons finely chopped celery	¼	teaspoon salt
2	tablespoons sweet pickle relish	¼	teaspoon sugar
3	tablespoons mayonnaise	¼	teaspoon freshly ground pepper
1	tablespoon grated onion	½	cup sliced pimiento-stuffed green olives
¾	teaspoon dried salad seasoning	6	bread slices

1. Mash 3 eggs in a large bowl using a fork or pastry blender. Chop remaining 3 eggs. Add chopped eggs, celery, and next 8 ingredients to mashed eggs; stir until blended. Gently stir in olives. Cover and chill, if desired. Divide egg salad among 3 bread slices; top with remaining bread slices. **Yield:** 3 sandwiches.

If you'd like to serve these sandwiches as smaller **finger sandwiches,** then freeze the bread for 10 to 15 minutes for easier cutting.

Chicken Pot Pie

prep: 20 min. • cook: 14 min. • bake: 30 min.

A rich, flaky browned crust beckons you to dive into this comfort meal.
Serving individual pot pies makes dinner an occasion.

one-dish meal • portable

½	cup butter	1	small onion, chopped
½	cup all-purpose flour	1	cup frozen green peas
1½	cups chicken broth	3½	cups chopped cooked chicken
1½	cups half-and-half	2	hard-cooked eggs, chopped
¾	teaspoon salt	1	(14.1-ounce) package refrigerated
½	teaspoon freshly ground pepper		piecrusts
2	tablespoons butter	1	tablespoon whipping cream
1	(8-ounce) package sliced fresh mushrooms	1	large egg, lightly beaten

1. Melt ½ cup butter in a heavy saucepan over low heat; whisk in flour, whisking until smooth. Cook, whisking constantly, 1 minute. Gradually add chicken broth and half-and-half; cook over medium heat, stirring constantly, until thickened and bubbly. Stir in ¾ teaspoon salt and ½ teaspoon pepper; set white sauce aside.

2. Melt 1 tablespoon butter in a large skillet over medium-high heat; add mushrooms, season lightly with salt and pepper, and sauté 10 minutes or until nicely browned. Don't overstir. Add mushrooms to white sauce. Add remaining 1 tablespoon butter to skillet. Add onion; sauté until tender. Stir in peas. Add vegetable mixture, chicken, and chopped eggs to white sauce.

3. Preheat oven to 375°. Fit 1 piecrust into a 9-inch deep-dish pie plate according to package directions. Spoon filling into crust; top with remaining piecrust. Trim off excess pastry. Fold edges under, and flute. Cut slits in top. Combine cream and egg; brush egg wash over pastry.

4. Bake at 375° for 30 to 40 minutes or until browned and bubbly. **Yield:** 6 servings.

Note: To make individual pot pies, spoon filling into 6 lightly greased 1-cup baking dishes. Cut out 6 circles of piecrust dough slightly larger than diameter of baking dishes. Top each dish with a round of dough; fold edges under, and flute. Cut slits in tops. Brush with egg wash. Bake at 375° for 30 to 35 minutes or until browned and bubbly.

Parmesan Chicken Salad

prep: 10 min. • cook: 14 min.

When you blend Parmesan, garlic, toasted pecans, and spicy brown mustard with chopped chicken, you get one fabulous chicken salad. It's even better the second day.

4	skinned and boned chicken breasts		½	cup chopped celery
1	teaspoon salt		⅓	cup chopped green onions
½	teaspoon pepper		¾	cup mayonnaise
2	tablespoons vegetable oil		2	tablespoons spicy brown mustard
¾	cup freshly grated Parmesan cheese		1	garlic clove, pressed
½	cup chopped pecans, toasted		Garnish: curly leaf lettuce	

1. Sprinkle chicken with salt and pepper. Cook chicken in hot oil in a large skillet over medium-high heat 7 to 8 minutes on each side or until done; cool. Chop chicken.

2. Stir together chopped chicken, cheese, and next 3 ingredients.

3. Stir together mayonnaise, mustard, and garlic. Add to chicken salad; stir well. Cover and chill, if desired. Garnish serving plate, if desired. **Yield:** 4½ cups.

Grilled Beer-Cheese Sandwich

prep: 5 min. • cook: 6 min.

The common grilled cheese sandwich gets fancy with amber beer in the filling.

2   teaspoons butter, softened
2   bread slices

¼   cup Beer-Cheese Spread

1. Spread 1 teaspoon softened butter on 1 side of 2 bread slices. Place bread slices, buttered sides down, on wax paper. Spread Beer-Cheese Spread onto unbuttered side of 1 bread slice. Top with remaining bread slice, buttered side up. Cook sandwich in a nonstick skillet or on a griddle over medium heat 3 to 5 minutes on each side or until golden brown and cheese is melted. **Yield:** 1 sandwich.

Beer-Cheese Spread

prep: 15 min. • chill: 2 hr.

This easy recipe (a tasty cousin of pimiento cheese) makes a lot, but the spread can be frozen up to a month; thaw it overnight in the refrigerator. It fits perfectly into four 10-ounce ramekins for gift giving. Try the spread over French fries, hot dogs, and chili, too.

1   (2-pound) block sharp Cheddar cheese, shredded
1   small onion, minced
2   garlic cloves, minced
½   teaspoon hot sauce

¼   teaspoon ground red pepper
1   (12-ounce) bottle amber beer, at room temperature
Salt and pepper to taste
Garnish: fresh thyme sprig

1. Beat first 5 ingredients at low speed with a heavy-duty electric stand mixer until blended. Gradually add beer, beating until blended after each addition. Beat at medium-high speed 1 minute or until blended and creamy. Season with salt and pepper to taste. Cover and chill 2 hours. Garnish, if desired. Store in an airtight container in refrigerator up to 2 weeks. **Yield:** 5 cups.

Chicken-and-Wild Rice Salad

Chicken-and-Wild Rice Salad

prep: 15 min. • bake: 10 min.

1 cup chopped pecans
3 tablespoons soy sauce
3 tablespoons rice wine vinegar
2 tablespoons sesame oil
1 (8.8-ounce) pouch ready-to-serve whole grain brown and wild rice mix

3 cups shredded cooked chicken
1 cup diced red bell pepper
1 cup coarsely chopped watercress
¼ cup minced green onions
Pepper to taste

1. Preheat oven to 350°. Bake pecans in a single layer in a shallow pan 10 to 12 minutes or until toasted and fragrant, stirring halfway through.
2. Whisk together soy sauce, vinegar, and sesame oil in a large bowl.
3. Prepare brown and wild rice mix according to package directions. Stir chicken, next 3 ingredients, toasted pecans, and rice into soy sauce mixture. Add pepper. **Yield:** 6 servings.

Strawberry-Spinach Chicken Salad

prep: 20 min.

1 (6-ounce) package fresh baby spinach
2 cups sliced strawberries
1 cup diced nectarines
¾ cup diced English cucumber
½ cup sliced red onion
4 cups coarsely chopped grilled chicken breasts

1 (3.5-ounce) package roasted glazed pecan pieces
1 (8-ounce) bottle poppy seed dressing
½ cup sweetened dried cranberries
½ cup crumbled blue cheese

1. Toss together first 5 ingredients. Top with chopped chicken and pecan pieces. Stir together poppy seed dressing, cranberries, and crumbled blue cheese; serve with salad. **Yield:** 6 servings.

Greek Pizza

prep: 15 min. • bake: 12 min.

Greek salad ingredients merge with hummus on this innovative pizza that's packed with flavor.

1	(12-inch) prebaked pizza crust	½	cup chopped red onion
1	cup deli hummus	¾	cup coarsely crumbled feta cheese
1	pint grape tomatoes	2	tablespoons olive oil (optional)
1	cup pitted kalamata olives	1	tablespoon fresh oregano leaves (optional)
½	cup pepperoncini rings, drained		

1. Preheat oven to 450°. Spread crust with hummus. Arrange grape tomatoes and next 3 ingredients over pizza. Sprinkle with feta cheese.

2. Bake directly on oven rack at 450° for 12 to 14 minutes or until feta cheese is lightly browned. Drizzle with olive oil, and sprinkle with oregano before serving, if desired. **Yield:** 4 servings.

Note: For added depth of flavor, drizzle the tomatoes and chopped red onion with 1 tablespoon olive oil, and roast on a baking sheet at 475° for 8 to 10 minutes before adding to pizza.

> Don't be intimidated by this homemade pizza. The convenience of **store-bought crust** and **deli hummus** makes this recipe a cinch.

Chili-Style Spaghetti and Meatballs

prep: 20 min. • bake: 15 min. • cook: 20 min.

*Discover a new flavor direction for an old classic. If desired, freeze
leftovers in single servings: spaghetti, three meatballs, and sauce.*

1½ pounds ground round
1 tablespoon grated onion
1 teaspoon salt
1 teaspoon ground cumin
12 ounces uncooked spaghetti
1 tablespoon chili powder
2 teaspoons olive oil
1 (14½-ounce) can diced tomatoes, undrained

1 (14-ounce) can beef broth
1 (6-ounce) can tomato paste
1 (4.5-ounce) can chopped green chiles
1 (15-ounce) can black beans, rinsed and drained

Toppings: sour cream, shredded Cheddar cheese, chopped red onion

1. Preheat oven to 350°. Combine first 4 ingredients in a large bowl just until blended. Gently shape meat mixture into 18 (1½-inch) balls.

2. Place a lightly greased rack in an aluminum foil-lined broiler pan, and arrange meatballs on rack.

3. Bake at 350° for 15 minutes or until browned. (Centers will be slightly pink.)

4. Prepare spaghetti according to package directions. Keep warm.

5. Cook chili powder in hot oil in a Dutch oven over medium heat, stirring constantly, 2 minutes. Stir in tomatoes and next 3 ingredients. Gently stir meatballs into tomato mixture. Bring to a boil; cover, reduce heat, and simmer, stirring occasionally, 10 minutes. Gently stir in beans, and cook 3 more minutes. Serve immediately with spaghetti and desired toppings. **Yield:** 6 servings.

Slow-Cooker BBQ Pork

prep: 5 min. • cook: 6 hr.

This super-simple recipe delivers big flavor. Reduce the fat but not the flavor in this juicy cut of pork by preparing it a day ahead. Cool the barbecue, and refrigerate overnight. Remove and discard any solidified fat before reheating.

make ahead • slow cooker

1   (3- to 4-pound) shoulder pork roast
1   (18-ounce) bottle barbecue sauce

1   (12-ounce) can cola soft drink

1. Place pork roast in a 6-quart slow cooker; pour barbecue sauce and cola over roast.
2. Cover with lid, and cook on HIGH 6 to 7 hours or until meat is tender and shreds easily. Serve on buns with slaw or over hot toasted cornbread. **Yield:** 6 servings.

Note: We tested with Sticky Fingers Memphis Original Barbecue Sauce. If you don't have a slow cooker, place roast in a lightly greased Dutch oven; stir together barbecue sauce and cola, and pour over roast. Before placing lid on top of Dutch oven, cover roast with a double layer of aluminum foil. Bake, tightly covered, at 325° for 3½ hours or until tender.

Memphis-Style Coleslaw

prep: 7 min. • chill: 2 hr.

make ahead

2   cups mayonnaise
¼   cup sugar
¼   cup Dijon mustard
¼   cup cider vinegar
1½   to 2 tablespoons celery seeds
1   teaspoon salt

⅛   teaspoon pepper
1   medium cabbage, shredded, or 3 (10-ounce) bags finely shredded cabbage
2   large carrots, grated
1   green bell pepper, diced
2   tablespoons grated onion

1. Stir together first 7 ingredients in a large bowl; add cabbage and remaining ingredients, tossing gently. Cover and chill 2 to 3 hours; serve with a slotted spoon. **Yield:** 12 servings.

Cola Pot Roast

prep: 30 min. • chill: 8 hr. • cook: 12 min. • bake: 4 hr.

Instead of broth, cola is used for cooking this roast. It adds a slightly sweet flavor note to the meat and vegetables. Grind some fresh pepper over the roast before serving, if desired.

1 (12-ounce) can cola soft drink
1 medium onion, chopped
8 garlic cloves, minced
1 lemon, thinly sliced
1 cup soy sauce
3 tablespoons vegetable oil, divided
1 (3- to 4-pound) boneless chuck roast, trimmed
1 teaspoon fresh coarsely ground pepper
8 large carrots (about 1½ pounds), cut into 1½-inch chunks
7 Yukon gold potatoes (about 2¼ pounds), cut into quarters
2 large onions, cut into eighths
2 tablespoons cornstarch
Garnish: fresh oregano or thyme sprigs

1. Combine first 5 ingredients and 2 tablespoons oil in a large zip-top plastic freezer bag. Add roast, turning to coat. Seal and chill 8 to 24 hours. Remove roast from marinade; discard lemon slices, and reserve marinade. Sprinkle roast with pepper.

2. Brown roast 4 minutes on each side in remaining 1 tablespoon hot oil in a large skillet over medium-high heat. Remove roast from skillet, and transfer to a large roasting pan. Add reserved marinade to skillet, stirring to loosen particles from bottom. Bring to a boil. Remove from heat.

3. Preheat oven to 300°. Arrange carrots, potatoes, and onions around roast in pan; pour hot marinade over roast and vegetables. Cover and bake at 300° for 4 hours or until meat and vegetables are tender. Transfer roast and vegetables to a serving platter. Skim fat from juices in roasting pan.

4. Whisk together cornstarch and ½ cup cold water in a small bowl until smooth. Whisk cornstarch mixture into juices in pan; cook over medium-high heat 3 minutes or until thickened, whisking to loosen particles. Serve gravy with roast and vegetables. Garnish, if desired. **Yield:** 6 to 8 servings.

Chicken-Fried Steak

prep: 10 min. • cook: 42 min.

Authentic chicken-fried steak is crunchy outside, tender inside, and served with plenty of cream gravy made from pan drippings. Bring it on!

2¼	teaspoons salt, divided
¼	teaspoon ground black pepper
6	(4-ounce) cube steaks
38	saltine crackers (1 sleeve), crushed
1¼	cups all-purpose flour, divided
½	teaspoon baking powder

1½	teaspoons ground black pepper, divided
½	teaspoon ground red pepper
4¾	cups milk, divided
2	large eggs
3½	cups peanut oil

1. Sprinkle ¼ teaspoon each salt and black pepper over steaks. Set aside.

2. Combine cracker crumbs, 1 cup flour, baking powder, 1 teaspoon salt, ½ teaspoon black pepper, and red pepper.

3. Whisk together ¾ cup milk and eggs. Dredge steaks in cracker crumb mixture; dip in milk mixture, and dredge in cracker mixture again.

4. Preheat oven to 225°. Pour oil into a 12-inch skillet; heat to 360°. (Do not use a nonstick skillet.) Fry steaks, in batches, 10 minutes. Turn and fry each batch 4 to 5 more minutes or until golden brown. Remove to a wire rack on a jelly-roll pan. Keep steaks warm in a 225° oven. Carefully drain hot oil, reserving cooked bits and 1 tablespoon drippings in skillet.

5. Whisk together remaining ¼ cup flour, 1 teaspoon salt, 1 teaspoon black pepper, and 4 cups milk. Pour mixture into reserved drippings in skillet; cook over medium-high heat, whisking constantly, 10 to 12 minutes or until thickened. Serve gravy with steaks and mashed potatoes.
Yield: 6 servings.

" Chicken-fried steak might just well be the state dish of **Texas.** Dinner plates laden with fried steaks, **potatoes, and gravy** are as much a part of the Lone Star State's persona as tumbleweeds and cowboy hats. "

Pan-Fried Pork Chops

prep: 10 min. • cook: 2 min. per batch

½ cup all-purpose flour
1 teaspoon salt
1 teaspoon seasoned pepper

1½ pounds wafer-thin boneless pork chops
¼ cup vegetable oil

1. Combine first 3 ingredients in a shallow dish; dredge pork chops in flour mixture.
2. Fry pork chops, in 3 batches, in hot oil in a large skillet over medium-high heat 1 minute on each side or until browned. Drain on paper towels. **Yield:** 6 to 8 servings.

Chicken and Dumplings

prep: 15 min. • cook: 25 min.

Deli-roasted chicken and canned biscuits make a tasty speed-scratch version of this familiar old favorite. One roasted chicken yields about three cups of meat.

1   (32-ounce) container low-sodium chicken broth
1   (14½-ounce) can low-sodium chicken broth
3   cups shredded cooked chicken (about 1½ pounds)
1   (10¾-ounce) can reduced-fat cream of celery soup

¼   teaspoon poultry seasoning
2   hard-cooked eggs, chopped
1   (10.2-ounce) can refrigerated jumbo buttermilk biscuits
Garnish: chopped fresh parsley

one-dish meal

1. Stir together first 5 ingredients in a Dutch oven over medium-high heat; bring to a boil. Reduce heat to low; simmer, stirring occasionally, 15 minutes. Add chopped eggs.
2. Place biscuits on a lightly floured surface. Roll or pat each biscuit to ⅛-inch thickness; cut into ½-inch-wide strips.
3. Return broth mixture to a low boil over medium-high heat. Drop strips, 1 at a time, into boiling broth. Reduce heat to low; simmer 10 minutes, stirring occasionally to prevent dumplings from sticking. Garnish, if desired. **Yield:** 4 to 6 servings.

> Southern cooks in a hurry have been known to make dumplings from frozen or canned **biscuits** as in this recipe. And though these doughy kinds have been labeled "Yankee dumplings" by some, any true **Southerner** would be happy to accept a bowlful.

Pork Chops, Cabbage, and Apples

prep: 20 min. • cook: 49 min.

Pork, cabbage, and apples make a classic combination that's really delightful.

3 teaspoons paprika, divided	1 head cabbage (about 2 pounds), coarsely chopped
2 teaspoons chopped fresh or 1 teaspoon dried thyme, divided	2 medium onions, thinly sliced
2 teaspoons kosher salt, divided	1 large Granny Smith apple, peeled and sliced
1½ teaspoons freshly ground pepper, divided	1 tablespoon tomato paste
2 teaspoons chopped fresh or 1 teaspoon dried sage, divided	1 (12-ounce) bottle lager beer*
6 (½-inch-thick) bone-in pork loin chops	Garnish: fresh thyme sprigs
2 bacon slices	

1. Combine 2 teaspoons paprika, 1 teaspoon fresh or ½ teaspoon dried thyme, 1 teaspoon salt, 1 teaspoon pepper, and 1 teaspoon fresh or ½ teaspoon dried sage; rub over pork chops.

2. Cook bacon slices in a large, deep skillet over medium-high heat 6 to 8 minutes or until crisp; remove bacon, and drain on paper towels, reserving drippings in skillet. Crumble bacon. Cook pork in hot drippings 3 minutes on each side or until browned and done; remove pork from skillet, and keep warm.

3. Add cabbage, onions, and apple to skillet. Cover and reduce heat to medium; cook, stirring occasionally, 15 minutes or until cabbage begins to wilt. Add tomato paste, beer, bacon, remaining 1 teaspoon paprika, 1 teaspoon fresh or ½ teaspoon dried thyme, 1 teaspoon salt, ½ teaspoon pepper, and 1 teaspoon fresh or ½ teaspoon dried sage, stirring to loosen particles from bottom of skillet. Cover and cook 15 minutes or until cabbage is tender and liquid is slightly thickened. Add pork, and cook, uncovered, 5 minutes or until thoroughly heated. Garnish, if desired. **Yield:** 6 servings.

*1½ cups apple cider may be substituted for the beer.

Fried Lemon-Rosemary Catfish

prep: 10 min. • chill: 1 hr. • cook: 8 min.

Fresh herb flavor and a squirt of citrus send fried catfish uptown. You can still add tartar sauce.

1	large lemon	4	(4- to 6-ounce) catfish fillets
¼	cup milk	2	cups yellow cornmeal
2	medium eggs, beaten	¼	cup olive oil
2	tablespoons chopped fresh rosemary		Garnishes: lemon wedges, fresh rosemary
2	tablespoons minced fresh garlic		sprigs

1. Grate zest from lemon, avoiding the pale bitter pith, into a large bowl; squeeze lemon juice into bowl. Stir in milk and next 3 ingredients until blended.

2. Rinse fillets, and pat dry with paper towels. Add fillets to lemon mixture in bowl; cover and chill 1 hour.

3. Place cornmeal on a large plate or in a large shallow dish. Turn fillets in lemon mixture until thoroughly coated; dredge in cornmeal, coating evenly.

4. Cook fillets in hot oil in a large skillet over medium-high heat 4 minutes on each side or until browned. Remove from skillet. Garnish, if desired. **Yield:** 4 servings.

To keep catfish **warm,** place fried fish on a wire rack with an aluminum foil-lined pan underneath; place in a 250° oven. For a **crisp texture,** do not cover fillets.

BLT Potato Salad

prep: 20 min. • cook: 15 min. • chill: 3 hr.

Potato salad—pure and simple—remains one of the tastiest icons of a Southern picnic. Merging it with the flavors of a BLT is a real treat.

3   large baking potatoes (about 3½ pounds), peeled and chopped
1   cup mayonnaise
3   tablespoons sweet pickle relish
2   tablespoons Dijon mustard
¼   cup chopped fresh flat-leaf parsley
1   teaspoon salt

1   teaspoon freshly ground pepper
4   green onions, sliced
2   hard-cooked eggs, coarsely chopped
1   cup grape tomatoes, halved
8   bacon slices, cooked and crumbled
Curly leaf lettuce leaves

1. Bring potatoes and salted water to cover to a boil in a Dutch oven. Boil 15 to 20 minutes or until tender (do not overcook). Drain and cool.

2. Stir together mayonnaise and next 5 ingredients in a large bowl; add cooked potatoes, green onions, and eggs, tossing gently until well blended. Gently stir in tomatoes. Cover and chill at least 3 hours. Stir in bacon just before serving. Serve on lettuce leaves. **Yield:** 8 to 10 servings.

Picnic Potato Salad

prep: 20 min. • cook: 40 min. • cool: 15 min. • chill: 12 hr.

4   pounds Yukon gold potatoes
3   hard-cooked eggs, grated
1   cup mayonnaise
½   cup diced celery
½   cup sour cream

⅓   cup finely chopped sweet onion
¼   cup sweet pickle relish
1   tablespoon spicy brown mustard
1   teaspoon salt
¾   teaspoon freshly ground pepper

1. Cook potatoes in boiling water to cover 40 minutes or until tender; drain and cool 15 minutes. Peel potatoes, and cut into 1-inch cubes.

2. Combine potatoes and eggs.

3. Stir together mayonnaise and next 7 ingredients; gently stir into potato mixture. Serve immediately, or cover and chill 12 hours. **Yield:** 8 servings.

BLT Potato Salad

Pimiento Cheese Panini

prep: 15 min. • cook: 3 min. per batch

It's tough to deny the simple pleasure of this classic cheese spread, especially when it's slathered onto crusty peasant bread and then grilled.

¾ cup mayonnaise

1 (4-ounce) jar diced pimiento, drained

1 teaspoon Worcestershire sauce

1 teaspoon finely grated onion

¼ teaspoon ground red pepper

1 (8-ounce) block extra-sharp Cheddar cheese, finely shredded

1 (8-ounce) block sharp Cheddar cheese, shredded

2 medium jalapeño peppers, seeded and minced (optional)

2 (16-ounce) loaves ciabatta bread

Olive oil

1. Stir together first 5 ingredients in a large bowl; stir in cheeses and, if desired, jalapeño. Store in refrigerator up to 1 week.

2. Slice bread into 20 (½-inch-thick) diagonal slices. Spread half of slices with pimiento cheese. Top with remaining slices. Brush outside of bread slices with olive oil.

3. Preheat panini press. Grill sandwiches, in batches, 3 to 4 minutes or until golden brown and cheese is melted. Cut sandwiches in half, if desired. **Yield:** 10 sandwiches.

These **melt-in-your-mouth** sandwiches pair perfectly with a bowl of tomato soup.

Mama's Fried Chicken

prep: 30 min. • chill: 2 hr. • cook: 26 min. per batch

1 (3- to 4-pound) whole chicken, cut into pieces	2 cups buttermilk
1 teaspoon salt	Self-rising flour
1 teaspoon pepper	Vegetable oil
	Salt (optional)

1. Sprinkle chicken with 1 teaspoon each salt and pepper. Place chicken in a shallow dish or zip-top plastic freezer bag, and add buttermilk. Cover or seal, and chill at least 2 hours.
2. Remove chicken from buttermilk, discarding buttermilk. Dredge chicken in flour. Pour oil to a depth of 1½ inches in a deep skillet or Dutch oven; heat to 360°. Add chicken, a few pieces at a time; cover and cook 6 minutes. Uncover chicken, and cook 9 minutes. Turn chicken; cover and cook 6 minutes. Uncover and cook 5 to 9 minutes, turning chicken the last 3 minutes for even browning, if necessary. Drain on paper towels. Sprinkle lightly with salt while chicken is hot, if desired. **Yield:** 4 to 6 servings.

"Fried" Pecan Chicken Fingers

prep: 10 min. • bake: 30 min.

Serve with your choice of barbecue sauce, Ranch dressing, or spicy-sweet honey mustard.

1 cup pecan halves	2 large eggs
1½ cups all-purpose baking mix	½ cup buttermilk
1 teaspoon salt	Vegetable cooking spray
½ teaspoon pepper	Garnish: green onion curls
1 (18.4-ounce) package boneless, skinless chicken breast tenderloins	

1. Preheat oven to 350°. Place pecans in a single layer in a shallow pan. Bake at 350° for 10 minutes or until lightly toasted, stirring occasionally. Increase oven temperature to 425°.
2. Process toasted pecans, baking mix, salt, and pepper in a food processor until pecans are finely ground. Place ½ cup pecan mixture in a large bowl. Add chicken, tossing to coat.
3. Whisk together eggs and buttermilk. Dip chicken in milk mixture; dredge in remaining pecan mixture. Arrange chicken in a single layer on a lightly greased aluminum foil-lined baking sheet. Lightly coat tops of chicken with cooking spray.
4. Bake at 425° for 20 to 25 minutes or until chicken is golden brown. Arrange on a serving platter, and garnish, if desired. **Yield:** 6 to 8 servings.

Mama's Fried Chicken

Caramel Cake

prep: 15 min. • bake: 30 min. • cool: 1 hr., 10 min.

1	(8-ounce) container sour cream	2¾	cups all-purpose flour
¼	cup milk	2	teaspoons baking powder
1	cup butter, softened	½	teaspoon salt
2	cups sugar	1	teaspoon vanilla extract
4	large eggs		Caramel Frosting

1. Preheat oven to 350°. Combine sour cream and milk. Beat butter at medium speed with an electric mixer until creamy; gradually add sugar, beating well. Add eggs, 1 at a time, beating after each addition.

2. Combine flour, baking powder, and salt; add to butter mixture alternately with sour cream mixture, beginning and ending with flour mixture. Beat at medium-low speed until blended after each addition. Stir in vanilla. Pour batter into 2 greased and floured 9-inch round cake pans.

3. Bake at 350° for 30 to 35 minutes or until a wooden pick inserted in center comes out clean. Let cool in pans on wire racks 10 minutes. Remove from pans to wire racks, and cool completely (about 1 hour). Spread Caramel Frosting between layers and on top and sides of cake. **Yield:** 8 servings.

Caramel Frosting

prep: 30 min. • cook: 20 min. • cool: 1 hr.

⅓	cup sugar	1	cup milk
1	tablespoon all-purpose flour	¾	cup butter
2½	cups sugar	1	teaspoon vanilla extract

1. Sprinkle ⅓ cup sugar in a shallow, heavy 3½-quart Dutch oven; cook over medium heat, stirring constantly, 3 minutes or until sugar is melted and syrup is light golden brown (sugar will clump). Remove from heat. Stir together 1 tablespoon flour and 2½ cups sugar in a large saucepan; add milk, and bring to a boil over medium-high heat, stirring constantly.

2. Gradually pour about one-fourth hot milk mixture into caramelized sugar, stirring constantly; gradually stir in remaining hot milk mixture until smooth. (Mixture will lump, but continue stirring until smooth.)

3. Cover and cook over low heat 2 minutes. Increase heat to medium; uncover and cook, without stirring, until a candy thermometer reaches 238° (soft ball stage, about 10 minutes). Add butter, stirring until blended. Remove from heat, and let stand, without stirring, until temperature drops to 110° (about 1 hour).

4. Pour into bowl of a heavy-duty electric stand mixer. Add vanilla, and beat at medium speed with whisk attachment until spreading consistency (about 20 minutes). **Yield:** 3 cups.

Note: We tested with a KitchenAid 300-watt Ultra Power heavy-duty electric stand mixer.

Uptown Banana Pudding Cheesecake

prep: 25 min. • bake: 56 min. • chill: 8 hr.

1½ cups finely crushed vanilla wafers	3 (8-ounce) packages cream cheese, softened
¼ cup chopped walnuts, toasted	1 cup granulated sugar
¼ cup butter, melted	3 large eggs
2 large ripe bananas, diced	1 tablespoon coffee liqueur
1 tablespoon lemon juice	2 teaspoons vanilla extract
2 tablespoons light brown sugar	Meringue

1. Preheat oven to 350°. Combine first 3 ingredients in a small bowl. Press into bottom of a greased 9-inch springform pan. Bake at 350° for 10 minutes. Let cool on a wire rack.

2. Combine diced bananas and lemon juice in a small saucepan. Stir in brown sugar. Place over medium-high heat, and cook, stirring constantly, about 1 minute or just until sugar melts. Set banana mixture aside.

3. Beat cream cheese at medium speed with an electric mixer 3 minutes or until smooth. Gradually add granulated sugar, beating until blended. Add eggs, 1 at a time, beating until blended after each addition. Beat in liqueur and vanilla. Pour into prepared pan. Spoon tablespoonfuls of banana mixture over top, and swirl gently into batter.

4. Bake at 350° for 35 to 40 minutes or until center is almost set. Remove from oven, and increase oven temperature to 400°.

5. Drop spoonfuls of Meringue gently over hot cheesecake. Bake at 400° for 10 minutes or until Meringue is golden brown. Remove from oven, and gently run a knife around edge of cheesecake to loosen. Cool cheesecake completely in pan on a wire rack. Cover loosely, and chill 8 hours. Store in refrigerator. **Yield:** 10 to 12 servings.

Meringue

prep: 11 min.

3 egg whites	6 tablespoons sugar
¼ teaspoon salt	

1. Beat egg whites and salt at high speed with an electric mixer until foamy. Add sugar, 1 tablespoon at a time, beating until soft peaks form and sugar dissolves (about 1 to 2 minutes). **Yield:** about 2 cups.

Bananas Foster Upside-Down Coffee Cake

prep: 25 min. • bake: 53 min. • cool: 10 min.

½ cup chopped pecans
½ cup butter, softened and divided
2 tablespoons rum
1 cup firmly packed light brown sugar
2 medium-size ripe bananas
7 maraschino cherries
¾ cup granulated sugar, divided

2 large eggs, separated
¾ cup milk
½ cup sour cream
1 teaspoon vanilla extract
2 cups all-purpose baking mix
¼ teaspoon ground cinnamon
Whipped cream (optional)

1. Preheat oven to 350°. Bake chopped pecans in a single layer in a shallow pan 8 to 10 minutes or until toasted and fragrant, stirring after 5 minutes.

2. Melt ¼ cup butter in a 10-inch cast-iron skillet over low heat; stir in rum. Sprinkle brown sugar over rum mixture. Remove from heat.

3. Sprinkle pecans over brown sugar mixture. Cut bananas in half crosswise; cut each half lengthwise into 3 slices. Arrange banana slices in a spoke pattern over pecans. Cut 6 maraschino cherries in half. Place 1 cherry half between each banana slice. Place remaining whole cherry in center of skillet.

4. Beat remaining ¼ cup butter and ½ cup granulated sugar at medium speed with an electric mixer until blended. Add egg yolks, 1 at a time, beating just until blended after each addition. Add milk, sour cream, and vanilla, beating just until blended.

5. Combine baking mix and cinnamon. Add cinnamon mixture to sour cream mixture, beating just until blended.

6. Beat egg whites at high speed until soft peaks form. Gradually beat in remaining ¼ cup granulated sugar until stiff peaks form. Fold into batter. Spread batter over bananas in skillet.

7. Bake at 350° for 45 to 50 minutes or until a wooden pick inserted in center comes out clean. Let cool in skillet on a wire rack 10 minutes. Invert cake onto a serving plate. Serve warm with whipped cream, if desired. **Yield:** 8 to 10 servings.

Cherry Bread Pudding

prep: 25 min. • bake: 30 min. • stand: 40 min.

As it bakes, bread pudding will rise to the tops of the ramekins and may overflow. It will deflate once it's removed from oven.

1   (8-ounce) French bread loaf, cut into 1-inch pieces
Vegetable cooking spray
2   cups fat-free milk
½   (12-ounce) can evaporated fat-free milk
¾   cup no-calorie sweetener
¾   cup egg substitute

¼   cup sugar
1   tablespoon butter, melted
1   teaspoon vanilla extract
½   teaspoon ground cinnamon
¼   teaspoon ground nutmeg
Cherry Sauce

1. Preheat oven to 350°. Place bread pieces in 6 (8-ounce) ramekins coated with cooking spray. Place ramekins on a baking sheet.

2. Whisk together milk and next 8 ingredients until blended. Pour milk mixture over bread in ramekins; let stand 30 minutes, pressing bread to absorb mixture after 15 minutes.

3. Bake at 350° for 30 to 35 minutes or just until a knife inserted in center comes out clean. Let stand 10 minutes. Spoon Cherry Sauce over bread pudding. **Yield:** 6 servings.

Note: We tested with Splenda No Calorie Sweetener, Granulated.

Cherry Sauce

prep: 5 min. • cook: 16 min.

1   (15-ounce) can pitted tart cherries in water
3   tablespoons light brown sugar

2   tablespoons cherry-flavored liqueur

1. Combine all ingredients in a small saucepan. Cook over medium-high heat, stirring occasionally, 16 to 18 minutes or until most of the liquid is reduced. **Yield:** about 1 cup

Waffles Benedict, page 103

breakfast anytime

Nutty Granola

prep: 4 min. • bake: 25 min.

Enjoy this healthy snack sprinkled over yogurt for breakfast.

3	cups uncooked regular oats
½	cup flaked coconut or organic coconut chips
½	cup whole natural almonds
¼	cup regular or honey-crunch wheat germ
¼	cup sunflower kernels

¼	cup plus 2 tablespoons honey
¼	cup vegetable oil
2	tablespoons brown sugar
1	teaspoon vanilla extract
¼	teaspoon salt
¾	cup raisins

1. Preheat oven to 350°. Combine first 5 ingredients in a large bowl; stir well, and set aside.

2. Combine honey and next 4 ingredients; pour over oats mixture, and stir well. Spread granola mixture onto a lightly greased 15- x 10-inch jelly-roll pan.

3. Bake at 350° for 25 minutes or until golden, stirring every 5 minutes. Cool. Stir in raisins. Store in an airtight container in a cool, dry place up to 1½ months. **Yield:** 5½ cups.

Mixed Fruit Granola

prep: 10 min. • cook: 5 min. • bake: 25 min.

make ahead

3	cups uncooked regular oats		½	cup butter
¼	cup wheat germ		½	cup firmly packed brown sugar
¼	cup sunflower seed kernels		2	tablespoons corn syrup
¼	cup chopped pecans		1	teaspoon vanilla extract
2	tablespoons sesame seeds		1	cup chopped dried mixed fruit

1. Preheat oven to 350°. Combine first 5 ingredients in a bowl. Set oats mixture aside. Cook butter and brown sugar in a medium saucepan over medium heat, stirring constantly, until butter is melted and sugar is dissolved. Stir in corn syrup. Remove from heat, and stir in vanilla.
2. Pour sugar mixture evenly over oats mixture, tossing to coat well. Spread mixture evenly in a lightly greased jelly-roll or broiler pan.
3. Bake at 350° for 25 to 30 minutes, stirring 3 times. Cool completely. Stir in dried fruit. Store in an airtight container up to 2 weeks. **Yield:** about 4 cups.

This makes a good **high-fiber** snack for a great pick-me-up. Serve it with cereal or yogurt for a flavorful, healthy breakfast.

Farmers' Market Scramble

Farmers' Market Scramble

prep: 10 min. • cook: 14 min.

Fresh herbs and tomato give these eggs a punch of flavor.

12	large eggs	2	tablespoons butter
¼	cup milk	1	tomato, chopped and drained on a paper towel
¼	cup whipping cream		
¾	teaspoon salt	¼	cup chopped fresh chives
¼	teaspoon freshly ground pepper	2	tablespoons chopped fresh flat-leaf parsley
¼	teaspoon hot sauce		

1. Whisk together first 6 ingredients in a large bowl until blended.
2. Melt 2 tablespoons butter in a large nonstick skillet over medium heat. Add egg mixture; cook, without stirring, until eggs begin to set on bottom. Draw a spatula across bottom of skillet to form large curds. Cook until eggs are thickened but still moist. (Do not stir constantly.)
3. Remove from heat, and transfer to a warm platter. Sprinkle platter of eggs with tomato, chives, and parsley; serve hot. **Yield:** 6 servings.

Smoky Brown Sugar Bacon

prep: 12 min. • bake: 20 min. per batch

This bacon takes a little while to prepare, but it's more than worth it. Any bacon left after breakfast makes for primo sandwiches.

3	cups firmly packed light brown sugar	24	slices applewood smoked bacon

1. Preheat oven to 425°. Spread brown sugar onto a large plate; dredge half of bacon in sugar, pressing to be sure plenty of sugar sticks to both sides of bacon. Place bacon in a single layer on a large wire rack on an aluminum foil-lined rimmed baking sheet.
2. Bake at 425° for 18 to 20 minutes or until crisp. Remove bacon from rack to a serving platter or parchment paper to cool. Repeat with remaining bacon and brown sugar. **Yield:** 24 slices.

Note: We used 1½ (1-pound) packages Nueske's Applewood Smoked Bacon to yield the 24 slices; otherwise, any thick-cut bacon, smoked or not, would also work well in this recipe.

Sausage-and-Egg Casserole

prep: 20 min. • bake: 1 hr.

Use 1 (16-ounce) package of crumbled pork sausage instead of the patties, if desired. Simply cook in a nonstick skillet until browned and crumbled.

make ahead

8 (1½-ounce) sourdough bread slices, cut into ½-inch cubes
1 (12-ounce) package fully cooked pork sausage patties, chopped
2½ cups 2% reduced-fat milk
4 large eggs

1 tablespoon Dijon mustard
½ cup buttermilk
1 (10¾-ounce) can cream of mushroom soup
1 cup (4 ounces) shredded sharp Cheddar cheese

1. Preheat oven to 350°. Arrange bread in 2 lightly greased 8-inch square baking dishes or 1 lightly greased 13- x 9-inch baking dish. Top evenly with sausage. Whisk together 2½ cups milk, eggs, and Dijon mustard. Pour evenly over bread mixture.
2. Whisk together buttermilk and cream of mushroom soup. Spoon over bread mixture; sprinkle with Cheddar cheese. Place casserole on a baking sheet.
3. Bake at 350° for 1 hour or until casserole is set. Serve immediately. **Yield:** 10 servings.

Note: An unbaked casserole can be covered with plastic wrap, then foil, and frozen up to 1 month. Thaw overnight in the refrigerator. Bake as directed.

Fresh fruit makes a delicious accompaniment with this melt-in-your-mouth casserole that's **perfect** for a company breakfast or also as a weeknight supper.

Pimiento Cheese Biscuits

prep: 20 min. • chill: 10 min. • bake: 13 min.

Any Southerner would be proud to have a bowl of these piping hot cheese biscuits on the breakfast table.

1   cup (4 ounces) shredded sharp Cheddar cheese
2¼ cups self-rising soft-wheat flour
½   cup cold butter, cut into ¼-inch-thick slices

1   cup buttermilk
1   (4-ounce) jar diced pimiento, drained
Self-rising soft-wheat flour
2   tablespoons melted butter

1. Combine shredded cheese and 2¼ cups flour in a large bowl.

2. Sprinkle butter slices over flour-cheese mixture; toss gently. Cut butter into flour with a pastry blender until crumbly. Cover and chill 10 minutes.

3. Combine buttermilk and diced pimiento; add buttermilk mixture to flour mixture, stirring just until dry ingredients are moistened.

4. Turn dough out onto a lightly floured surface, and knead 3 or 4 times, gradually adding additional flour as needed. With floured hands, press or pat dough into a ¾-inch-thick rectangle (about 9 x 5 inches). Sprinkle top of dough with additional flour. Fold dough over onto itself in 3 sections, starting with 1 short end. (Fold dough rectangle as if folding a letter-size piece of paper.) Repeat procedure 2 more times, beginning with pressing into a ¾-inch-thick dough rectangle (about 9 x 5 inches).

5. Preheat oven to 450°. Press or pat dough to ½-inch thickness on a lightly floured surface; cut with a 2-inch round cutter, and place, side by side, on a parchment paper-lined or lightly greased jelly-roll pan. (Dough rounds should touch.)

6. Bake at 450° for 13 to 15 minutes or until lightly browned. Remove from oven, and brush with 2 tablespoons melted butter. **Yield:** 2½ dozen.

Ham-Stuffed Biscuits With Mustard Butter

prep: 1 hr. • bake: 10 min. • stand: 1 hr., 5 min.

1	(¼-ounce) envelope active dry yeast		½	teaspoon baking soda
½	cup warm water (100° to 110°)		¼	cup sugar
2	cups buttermilk		¾	cup shortening
5½	cups all-purpose flour			Mustard Butter
1½	tablespoons baking powder		2	pounds thinly sliced cooked ham
1½	teaspoons salt			

1. Combine yeast and ½ cup warm water in a 4-cup liquid measuring cup, and let mixture stand 5 minutes. Stir in buttermilk.

2. Combine flour and next 4 ingredients in a large bowl; cut in shortening with a pastry blender or fork until crumbly. Add buttermilk mixture, stirring with a fork just until dry ingredients are moistened.

3. Turn dough out onto a well-floured surface, and knead 4 to 5 times.

4. Roll dough to ½-inch thickness; cut with a 2-inch round cutter, and place on lightly greased baking sheets. Cover and let rise in a warm place (85°), free from drafts, 1 hour.

5. Preheat oven to 425°. Bake for 10 to 12 minutes or until golden. Split each biscuit, and spread evenly with Mustard Butter. Stuff biscuits with ham. **Yield:** 5 dozen.

Mustard Butter

prep: 5 min.

1	cup butter, softened		2	tablespoons spicy brown mustard
2	tablespoons minced sweet onion			

1. Stir together all ingredients until blended. **Yield:** about 1 cup.

Country Ham With Redeye Gravy

prep: 10 min. • cook: 25 min.

For true redeye gravy, Southerners use caffeinated coffee for its pick-me-up quality.

2   cups hot strong brewed coffee
¼   cup firmly packed brown sugar

2   (12-ounce) slices boneless country ham

1. Stir together coffee and sugar; let mixture cool.
2. Cook ham in a large cast-iron skillet over medium heat 5 to 7 minutes on each side or until browned. Remove ham, and keep warm, reserving drippings in skillet.
3. Add coffee mixture to skillet, stirring to loosen particles from bottom; bring to a boil. Boil, stirring occasionally, until reduced by half (about 15 minutes). Serve with ham. **Yield:** 6 servings.

Margaret's Creamy Grits

prep: 10 min. • cook: 10 min.

Former Test Kitchens Director Margaret Dickey had a knack for thick, rich grits.

2   cups half-and-half or whipping cream
¼   teaspoon salt
⅛   teaspoon granulated garlic
⅛   teaspoon pepper
½   cup uncooked quick-cooking grits

2   ounces cream cheese, cubed
¾   cup (3 ounces) shredded sharp Cheddar cheese
¼   teaspoon hot sauce

1. Bring first 4 ingredients to a boil in a Dutch oven; gradually stir in grits. Return to a boil; cover, reduce heat, and simmer, stirring occasionally, 5 to 7 minutes or until thickened. Add cheeses and hot sauce, stirring until cheeses melt. Serve hot. **Yield:** 4 servings.

Hash Brown Casserole

prep: 20 min. • bake: 1 hr.

This down-home side dish boasts a buttery cornflake crust on top.

¾ cup chopped onion
½ teaspoon paprika
½ teaspoon freshly ground pepper
1 (32-ounce) package frozen Southern-style hash brown potatoes (diced)
2 tablespoons butter, melted

1 (10¾-ounce) can cream of chicken soup
1 (8-ounce) package pasteurized prepared cheese product, cubed
1 (8-ounce) container sour cream
2½ cups cornflakes cereal, coarsely crushed
2 tablespoons butter, melted

1. Preheat oven to 350°. Combine first 5 ingredients in a large bowl; toss well.
2. Combine soup and cheese in a medium microwave-safe bowl. Microwave at HIGH 6 minutes or until cheese melts, stirring every 2 minutes. Stir in sour cream. Pour cheese mixture over potato mixture, and stir well. Spread into a lightly greased 13- x 9-inch baking dish.
3. Combine cornflakes and 2 tablespoons butter; sprinkle over top of potato mixture. Bake, uncovered, at 350° for 1 hour. **Yield:** 12 servings.

Country Breakfast Casserole

prep: 10 min. • cook: 10 min. • bake: 45 min. • stand: 5 min.

1 pound ground mild pork sausage
1 teaspoon salt
1 cup uncooked quick-cooking grits
1½ cups (6 ounces) shredded Cheddar cheese, divided

4 large eggs, lightly beaten
¾ cup milk
¼ cup butter, melted
¼ teaspoon pepper

1. Preheat oven to 350°. Brown sausage in a large skillet over medium heat, stirring until it crumbles and is no longer pink; drain.
2. Bring 3½ cups water and salt to a boil in a medium saucepan; stir in grits. Return to a boil; cover, reduce heat, and simmer 5 minutes, stirring occasionally. Remove from heat; add 1 cup cheese, stirring until cheese melts. Stir in sausage, eggs, and next 3 ingredients.
3. Pour mixture into a greased 11- x 7-inch baking dish; sprinkle with remaining ½ cup cheese.
4. Bake, uncovered, at 350° for 45 minutes or until set. Let stand 5 minutes before serving. **Yield:** 6 servings.

Hash Brown Casserole

Orange Rolls

Prep: 15 min. • Bake: 30 min.

Your family will definitely want to rise, shine, and dine when they smell these baking in the oven.

½ (8-ounce) package cream cheese, softened
¼ cup firmly packed light brown sugar
1½ teaspoons orange zest
1 (11-ounce) can refrigerated French bread dough

2 tablespoons granulated sugar
1 tablespoon butter, melted
½ cup powdered sugar
1 tablespoon orange juice

1. Preheat oven to 375°. Beat cream cheese, light brown sugar, and orange zest at medium speed with an electric mixer until smooth. Unroll French bread dough onto a lightly floured surface. Spread cream cheese mixture over dough, leaving a ¼-inch border. Sprinkle with granulated sugar. Gently roll up dough, starting at 1 long side. Cut into 11 (1¼-inch) slices.
2. Place slices in a lightly greased 8-inch round cake pan. Brush top of dough with melted butter. Bake 25 to 30 minutes or until golden. Stir together powdered sugar and orange juice in a small bowl until smooth. Drizzle over hot rolls. Serve immediately. **Yield:** 11 rolls.

Note: We tested with Pillsbury Crusty French Loaf.

These rolls are **easy to make** and taste just like they were made from scratch.

Cinnamon-Raisin Rolls

prep: 10 min. • stand: 30 min. • bake: 35 min.

These scrumptious breakfast rolls are made from a package of frozen biscuits. They're so easy to prepare, you don't even need a rolling pin.

1	(26.4-ounce) package frozen biscuits		1	cup golden raisins or raisins
	All-purpose flour		½	cup chopped pecans, toasted
¼	cup butter, softened		1	cup powdered sugar
¾	cup firmly packed brown sugar		3	tablespoons milk
1	teaspoon ground cinnamon		½	teaspoon vanilla extract

1. Arrange frozen biscuits, with sides touching, in 3 rows of 4 biscuits on a lightly floured surface. Let stand 30 to 45 minutes or until biscuits are thawed but still cool to the touch.

2. Preheat oven to 375°. Sprinkle thawed biscuits lightly with flour. Press biscuit edges together, and pat to form a 10- x 12-inch rectangle of dough; spread with softened butter. Stir together brown sugar and cinnamon; sprinkle over butter. Sprinkle raisins and pecans over brown sugar mixture.

3. Roll up dough, starting at 1 long end; cut into 12 (about 1-inch-thick) slices. Place rolls in a lightly greased 10-inch cast-iron skillet, 10-inch round pan, or 9-inch square pan. Bake at 375° for 35 to 40 minutes or until center rolls are golden brown and done; cool slightly.

4. Stir together powdered sugar, milk, and vanilla; drizzle over rolls. **Yield:** 1 dozen.

Note: For individual rolls, prepare as directed; place 1 slice in each of 12 lightly greased 3-inch muffin cups. Bake at 375° for 20 to 25 minutes or until golden brown. Cool slightly, and remove from pan. Drizzle with glaze.

make ahead • portable

Buttermilk 'n' Honey Pancakes

prep: 10 min. • cook: 2 min. per batch

Honey adds sweetness and moisture to these pancakes. Experiment by using dark or wildflower honey.

1	cup all-purpose flour		1	large egg, lightly beaten
1	teaspoon baking powder		1	cup buttermilk
½	teaspoon baking soda		2	tablespoons honey
¼	teaspoon salt			Pecan-Honey Butter (optional)

1. Stir together first 4 ingredients in a medium bowl. Add egg, buttermilk, and honey, stirring until well blended.

2. Pour ¼ cup batter onto a hot, lightly greased griddle or skillet. Cook 1 to 2 minutes or until top is covered with bubbles and edges look cooked. Turn and cook 1 more minute. Repeat with remaining batter. Top pancakes with Pecan-Honey Butter, if desired. Serve with syrup.
Yield: about 9 (3-inch) pancakes.

Note: For 5 jumbo pancakes, use a heaping ⅓ cup batter for each pancake.

Pecan-Honey Butter

prep: 5 min.

Let the chilled Pecan-Honey Butter stand at room temperature 10 to 15 minutes to soften before serving.

½	cup butter, softened		2	tablespoons honey
⅓	cup finely chopped pecans, toasted		⅛	to ¼ teaspoon ground cinnamon

1. Stir together all ingredients until blended. Cover and chill until ready to serve.
Yield: about ¾ cup.

Pam-Cakes With Buttered Honey Syrup

prep: 10 min. • cook: 24 min.

Use a light hand when stirring the batter; overmixing will cause a rubbery texture. When using a griddle to cook pancakes, set the temperature dial to 350°.

1¾	cups all-purpose flour	2	cups buttermilk
2	teaspoons sugar	2	large eggs
1½	teaspoons baking powder	¼	cup butter, melted
1	teaspoon baking soda		Buttered Honey Syrup
1	teaspoon salt		Garnish: fresh blueberries, apricots

1. Preheat oven to 200°. Combine first 5 ingredients in a large bowl. Whisk together buttermilk and eggs. Gradually stir buttermilk mixture into flour mixture. Gently stir in butter. (Batter will be lumpy.)
2. Pour about ¼ cup batter for each pancake onto a hot, buttered griddle or large nonstick skillet. Cook pancakes 3 to 4 minutes or until tops are covered with bubbles and edges look dry and cooked. Turn and cook 3 to 4 minutes or until golden brown. Place pancakes in a single layer on a baking sheet, and keep warm in a 200° oven up to 30 minutes. Serve with Buttered Honey Syrup. Garnish, if desired. **Yield:** about 16 (4-inch) pancakes.

Buttered Honey Syrup

prep: 5 min. • cook: 1 min.

⅓	cup butter	½	cup honey

1. Melt butter in a small saucepan over medium-low heat. Stir in honey, and cook 1 minute or until warm. **Yield:** about ¾ cup.

Note: Buttered Honey Syrup cannot be made ahead. The heated honey will crystallize when cooled and will not melt if reheated.

Blueberry Sweet Muffins

prep: 10 min. • bake: 20 min.

1½	cups all-purpose flour	¼	cup vegetable oil
½	cup sugar	1	large egg
2	teaspoons baking powder	1	cup fresh or frozen blueberries
½	teaspoon salt	2	tablespoons sugar
⅓	cup milk		

1. Preheat oven to 400°. Combine first 4 ingredients in a large bowl; make a well in center of mixture.

2. Stir together milk, oil, and egg; add to dry ingredients, stirring just until moistened. Fold in blueberries. Spoon into greased or paper-lined muffin pans, filling two-thirds full. Sprinkle batter with 2 tablespoons sugar.

3. Bake at 400° for 20 to 25 minutes or until muffins are golden. Remove from pans immediately, and cool on wire racks. **Yield:** 6 muffins.

Sour Cream Coffee Cake Muffins

prep: 20 min. • bake: 20 min. • cool: 12 min.

1	cup butter, softened	¼	teaspoon salt
2	cups sugar	⅛	teaspoon baking soda
2	large eggs	1	cup pecan halves, finely chopped
1	cup sour cream	¼	cup sugar
½	teaspoon vanilla extract	1½	teaspoons ground cinnamon
2	cups all-purpose flour		
1	teaspoon baking powder		

1. Preheat oven to 350°. Beat butter at medium speed with an electric mixer 2 minutes or until creamy. Gradually add 2 cups sugar, beating 2 to 3 minutes. Add eggs, 1 at a time, beating until blended after each addition. Add sour cream and vanilla, beating until blended.
2. Whisk together flour and next 3 ingredients; gradually stir into butter mixture. (Batter will be thick.)
3. Place baking cups in muffin pans. Spoon batter into cups, filling two-thirds full.
4. Stir together pecans, ¼ cup sugar, and cinnamon. Sprinkle pecan mixture over batter.
5. Bake at 350° for 20 to 25 minutes or until a wooden pick inserted in center comes out clean. Remove from pans, and cool completely on wire racks (about 12 to 15 minutes).
Yield: 24 muffins.

These **tasty little treats** also make a great gift. Simply leave the muffins in the muffin pan, wrap with cellophane, and tie with a festive ribbon.

Poppy Seed-Lemon Muffins

prep: 10 min. • bake: 18 min.

These are good on-the-go muffins, since they don't have a glaze. Rest assured, they're still plenty sweet.

1	(18.25-ounce) package yellow cake mix with pudding	4	large eggs
⅔	cup vegetable oil	⅓	cup poppy seeds
⅔	cup apricot nectar	½	teaspoon lemon zest
		2½	tablespoons fresh lemon juice

1. Preheat oven to 400°. Combine all ingredients, stirring until blended. Spoon into greased or paper-lined muffin pans, filling two-thirds full.
2. Bake at 400° for 18 to 20 minutes or until golden brown. Remove from pans immediately, and cool on wire racks. **Yield:** about 2 dozen.

Note: We tested with Betty Crocker Yellow Cake Mix with Pudding.

Oatmeal Muffins

prep: 12 min. • bake: 15 min.

Instead of having oatmeal for breakfast, try these tender oat muffins dotted with dates.

¾	cup all-purpose flour	½	teaspoon salt
1	cup uncooked regular oats	¾	cup milk
½	cup chopped dates	3	tablespoons butter, melted
¼	cup sugar	1	large egg, lightly beaten
1	tablespoon baking powder		Oats (optional)

1. Preheat oven to 425°. Combine first 6 ingredients in a large bowl; make a well in center of mixture. Stir together milk, butter, and egg; add to dry ingredients. Stir just until moistened.
2. Spoon batter into lightly greased or paper-lined muffin pans, filling two-thirds full. Sprinkle with oats, if desired.
3. Bake at 425° for 15 minutes. Remove from pans immediately. **Yield:** 8 muffins.

Note: We used 4-inch squares of parchment paper to fashion handmade paper muffin liners.

Poppy Seed-Lemon Muffins and Oatmeal Muffins

Banana Bread

prep: 15 min. • bake: 1 hr., 5 min. • cool: 10 min.

The best-tasting banana bread comes from using overripe bananas.
Yogurt adds a nice tang to this recipe.

2	cups self-rising flour	3	very ripe bananas, mashed (1½ cups)
1	cup sugar	2	large eggs, lightly beaten
¼	cup toasted wheat germ	¼	cup strawberry yogurt or vanilla yogurt
½	teaspoon baking soda	1½	teaspoons vanilla extract
½	cup butter, melted		

1. Preheat oven to 350°. Grease and flour a 9- x 5-inch loaf pan; set aside.

2. Combine first 4 ingredients in a large bowl; make a well in center of mixture. Stir together melted butter, mashed banana, eggs, yogurt, and vanilla. Add to dry ingredients; stir just until moistened. Pour batter into prepared pan.

3. Bake at 350° for 1 hour and 5 minutes or until a wooden pick inserted in center comes out clean. Cover loosely with aluminum foil after 40 minutes if loaf begins to brown too quickly. Cool in pan on a wire rack 10 minutes; remove from pan, and cool completely on wire rack. **Yield:** 1 loaf.

Note: For muffins, spoon batter into lightly greased or paper-lined muffin pans, filling three-fourths full. Bake at 350° for 19 to 21 minutes or until lightly browned. Remove from pans immediately. Let cool on wire racks. **Yield:** 20 muffins.

Variations

• **Banana-Nut Bread:** Add 1 cup chopped, toasted pecans to batter before baking.
• **Chocolate Chip-Banana Bread:** Add 1 cup semisweet chocolate morsels to batter before baking.

Chocolate Bread

prep: 21 min. • bake: 25 min. • stand: 3 hr., 15 min.

1¼	cups warm milk (100° to 110°)	1	teaspoon salt
½	cup warm water (100° to 110°)	1	large egg
1	(¼-ounce) envelope active dry yeast	2	tablespoons butter, softened
4½	cups all-purpose flour, divided	2	(4-ounce) semisweet chocolate bars, chopped
½	cup unsweetened cocoa		
¼	cup granulated sugar	1½	tablespoons turbinado sugar

1. Combine milk, ½ cup warm water, and yeast in a large bowl; whisk until smooth. Let stand 5 minutes. Stir 2 cups flour, cocoa, granulated sugar, and salt into yeast mixture; beat at medium speed with an electric mixer until smooth. Beat in egg, butter, and 2 cups flour until a soft dough forms.

2. Turn out dough onto a floured surface, and knead until smooth (about 6 minutes), adding remaining ½ cup flour, 1 tablespoon at a time as needed, to prevent dough from sticking. Fold in chopped chocolate during last minute of kneading.

3. Place dough in a large, lightly greased bowl, turning to coat top. Cover with plastic wrap, and let rise in a warm place (85°), free from drafts, 1 hour and 40 minutes or until doubled in bulk.

4. Punch dough down. Divide dough in half; gently shape each portion into an 8- x 4-inch oval. Place dough in 2 lightly greased 8½- x 4½-inch loaf pans. Cover and let rise 1½ hours or until doubled in bulk.

5. Preheat oven to 375°. Sprinkle loaves with turbinado sugar. Bake at 375° for 25 minutes or until loaves sound hollow when tapped. Remove from pans to wire racks, and let cool.

Yield: 2 loaves.

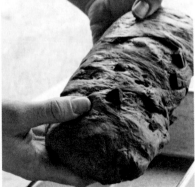

Fold/knead chopped chocolate into bread dough. Place dough in loaf pans to rise.

Waffles Benedict

prep: 15 min. • stand: 5 min. • cook: 20 min.

You can substitute prosciutto, deli ham, or country ham for the pancetta. Sauté it briefly for extra flavor.

2	cups all-purpose baking mix
1⅓	cups buttermilk
½	cup (2 ounces) shredded Parmesan cheese
2	tablespoons vegetable oil
9	large eggs
½	teaspoon white vinegar

1	(0.9-ounce) envelope hollandaise sauce mix
1	tablespoon lemon juice
½	teaspoon fresh or ¼ teaspoon dried tarragon
8	thin pancetta slices (about ¼ pound)
Garnish: chopped fresh chives	

1. Stir together first 4 ingredients and 1 egg in a medium bowl until blended. Let batter stand 5 minutes.

2. Meanwhile, add water to a depth of 3 inches in a large saucepan. Bring to a boil; reduce heat, and maintain a light simmer. Add vinegar. Working in 2 batches, break remaining 8 eggs, and slip into water, 1 at a time, as close as possible to surface. Simmer 3 to 5 minutes or to desired degree of doneness. Remove with a slotted spoon. Trim edges, if desired.

3. Cook batter in a preheated, lightly greased waffle iron according to manufacturer's directions until golden.

4. Prepare hollandaise sauce according to package directions, adding lemon juice and tarragon.

5. For each serving, stack 2 waffles, and top with 2 pancetta slices, 2 poached eggs, and desired amount of hollandaise sauce. Garnish, if desired. **Yield:** 4 servings.

Enjoy a twist on this **lavish dish** that uses waffles as the base rather than the traditional English muffin. It makes a **showstopping** brunch when paired with seasonal fruit.

Pecan Streusel Coffee Cake

prep: 17 min. • bake: 45 min.

A buttery coffee crumb mixture makes a shortbreadlike crust for this easy snack cake. This is one of the best coffee cakes around.

make ahead • portable

2 cups all-purpose flour
2 teaspoons instant coffee granules
2 cups firmly packed light brown sugar
1 teaspoon ground cinnamon
½ teaspoon salt

½ cup chilled butter, cut into pieces
1 (8-ounce) container sour cream
1 teaspoon baking soda
1 large egg, lightly beaten
1½ cups chopped pecans

1. Preheat oven to 350°. Combine flour and coffee granules in a large bowl. Add brown sugar, cinnamon, and salt; stir well. Cut in butter with a pastry blender until crumbly. Press half of crumb mixture into a greased 9-inch square pan; set aside.

2. Combine sour cream and baking soda, stirring well. Add to remaining crumb mixture, stirring just until dry ingredients are moistened. Add egg, stirring gently to combine. Pour sour cream mixture over crumb crust in pan; sprinkle with pecans.

3. Bake at 350° for 45 minutes. Cool and cut into squares. **Yield:** 1 (9-inch) coffee cake.

Serve this coffee cake for **breakfast**, or enjoy it with coffee for a scrumptious after-dinner **dessert**.

Apricot-Almond Coffee Cake

prep: 20 min. • cook: 25 min. • cool: 20 min.

4	ounces cream cheese, softened		2	large eggs
½	cup apricot preserves		½	teaspoon almond extract
1	(16-ounce) package pound cake mix, divided		½	cup sliced almonds
1	(8-ounce) container sour cream			Glaze
½	cup milk			

1. Preheat oven to 350°. Beat cream cheese, apricot preserves, and 1 tablespoon cake mix at medium-low speed with an electric mixer just until blended.

2. Beat sour cream, milk, eggs, almond extract, and remaining cake mix at low speed 30 seconds or until blended. Increase speed to medium, and beat 3 more minutes.

3. Pour sour cream batter into a lightly greased 13- x 9-inch pan. Dollop cream cheese mixture by rounded tablespoonfuls evenly over batter. Swirl batter gently with a knife. Sprinkle almonds over top.

4. Bake at 350° for 25 to 30 minutes or until light golden and a wooden pick inserted in center comes out clean. Let cool in pan on a wire rack 20 minutes. Drizzle Glaze over slightly warm cake or individual pieces. **Yield:** 15 servings.

Note: We tested with Betty Crocker Pound Cake Mix.

Glaze

prep: 5 min.

1	cup powdered sugar		1	to 2 tablespoons milk
½	teaspoon vanilla extract			

1. Stir together powdered sugar, vanilla, and 1 tablespoon milk in a small bowl until smooth. Stir in up to 1 tablespoon additional milk, if necessary, for desired consistency. **Yield:** ⅓ cup.

Brown Sugar-Pecan Coffee Cake

Brown Sugar-Pecan Coffee Cake

prep: 20 min. • bake: 25 min. • cool: 30 min.

2	cups all-purpose flour		1	teaspoon baking soda
2	cups firmly packed light brown sugar		3	tablespoons granulated sugar
¾	cup butter, cubed		1	teaspoon ground cinnamon
1	cup sour cream		1	cup chopped pecans
1	large egg, lightly beaten			

1. Preheat oven to 350°. Stir together flour and brown sugar in a large bowl. Cut ¾ cup butter into flour mixture with a pastry blender or 2 forks until crumbly. Press 2¾ cups crumb mixture evenly on the bottom of a lightly greased 13- x 9-inch pan.
2. Stir together sour cream, egg, and baking soda; add to remaining crumb mixture, stirring just until dry ingredients are moistened. Stir together granulated sugar and cinnamon. Pour sour cream mixture over crumb crust in pan; sprinkle evenly with cinnamon mixture and pecans.
3. Bake at 350° for 25 to 30 minutes or until a wooden pick inserted in center comes out clean. Let cool in pan on a wire rack 30 minutes. Serve warm. **Yield:** 12 servings.

Streusel-Spiced Coffee Cake

prep: 16 min. • bake: 35 min. • chill: 8 hr.

¾	cup unsalted butter, softened		½	teaspoon ground cinnamon
1	cup granulated sugar		½	teaspoon grated nutmeg
2	large eggs		½	teaspoon salt
1	cup sour cream		¾	cup firmly packed light brown sugar
2	cups all-purpose flour		1	cup coarsely chopped pecans
2	teaspoons baking powder		½	teaspoon ground cinnamon
1	teaspoon baking soda		¼	to ½ teaspoon grated nutmeg

1. Beat butter at medium speed with an electric mixer until fluffy; gradually add granulated sugar, beating well. Add eggs, 1 at a time, beating until blended after each addition. Add sour cream, mixing well.
2. Combine flour and next 5 ingredients; add to butter mixture, beating well. Spread batter into a greased and floured 13- x 9-inch pan.
3. Combine brown sugar, pecans, ½ teaspoon cinnamon, and ¼ to ½ teaspoon nutmeg in a small bowl. Sprinkle evenly over batter. Cover and refrigerate 8 hours.
4. Preheat oven to 350°. Remove pan from refrigerator, and uncover; bake at 350° for 35 minutes or until a wooden pick inserted in center comes out clean. **Yield:** 12 servings.

Almond French Toast

prep: 20 min. • stand: 5 min. • bake: 23 min.

Everyone needs an extravagant-tasting breakfast bread now and then. Bake this version in the oven instead of preparing it using the more involved stovetop method.

make ahead

6	(1-inch-thick) French bread slices	2	tablespoons almond liqueur (optional)
4	large eggs	3	tablespoons butter
½	cup milk	½	cup sliced almonds, toasted
1	tablespoon sugar		Powdered sugar
1	teaspoon almond extract		Maple syrup, warmed
½	teaspoon vanilla extract		

1. Arrange French bread slices in a 13- x 9-inch baking dish.

2. Whisk together eggs, next 4 ingredients, and, if desired, liqueur; pour over bread. Let stand 5 minutes, turning once. Cover and chill 8 hours, if desired.

3. Preheat oven to 400°. Melt butter at 400° in a 15- x 10-inch jelly-roll pan; add soaked bread slices.

4. Bake at 400° for 15 minutes; turn each slice, and bake 8 to 10 more minutes or until golden. Sprinkle with almonds and powdered sugar. Serve with maple syrup. **Yield:** 3 servings.

Fruit and whipped cream also make **delicious toppings** for this tasty breakfast favorite.

One-Dish Blackberry French Toast

prep: 21 min. • cook: 1 min. • bake: 30 min. • chill: 8 hr.

1   cup blackberry jam
1   (12-ounce) French bread loaf, cut into
    1½-inch cubes
1   (8-ounce) package ⅓-less-fat cream
    cheese, cut into 1-inch cubes
4   large eggs

2   cups half-and-half
1   teaspoon ground cinnamon
1   teaspoon vanilla extract
½   cup firmly packed brown sugar
Toppings: maple syrup, whipped cream

1. Cook jam in a small saucepan over medium heat 1 to 2 minutes or until melted and smooth, stirring once.

2. Place half of bread cubes in bottom of a lightly greased 13- x 9-inch baking dish. Top with cream cheese cubes, and drizzle with melted jam. Top with remaining bread cubes.

3. Whisk together eggs and next 3 ingredients. Pour over bread mixture. Sprinkle with brown sugar. Cover tightly, and chill 8 to 24 hours.

4. Preheat oven to 325°. Bake, covered, 20 minutes. Uncover and bake 10 to 15 minutes or until bread is golden brown and mixture is set. Serve with desired toppings. **Yield:** 8 to 10 servings.

"This dish also tastes great using **strawberry** jam. It's perfect to make the night before and just pop it into the oven in the morning."

Guiltless French Toast

Guiltless French Toast

prep: 16 min. • cook: 12 min.

8   egg whites
¼   cup fresh orange juice
1   tablespoon vanilla extract
1   teaspoon ground cinnamon

4   whole grain bakery bread slices
1   tablespoon butter
¼   cup maple syrup
Fresh blueberries and kiwi slices

1. Whisk together first 4 ingredients in a shallow dish. Dip bread slices in egg mixture, coating both sides.
2. Melt butter on a griddle or in a large nonstick skillet over medium heat. Place bread slices on hot griddle, and pour remaining egg mixture over bread slices. Cook 3 to 4 minutes on each side or until golden. Drizzle with maple syrup, and top with fruit. **Yield**: 4 servings.

Black Walnut French Toast

prep: 10 min. • cook: 12 min.

2   tablespoons chopped black walnuts
1   tablespoon butter
1   large ripe banana, sliced
¼   cup honey
2   large eggs, lightly beaten

¼   cup fat-free milk
½   teaspoon ground cinnamon
⅛   teaspoon ground nutmeg
8   (0.8-ounce) white bread slices
¼   cup reduced-calorie maple syrup

1. Place a small skillet over medium-high heat until hot; add 2 tablespoons chopped black walnuts, and cook, stirring constantly, 5 minutes or until toasted. Remove from skillet.
2. Melt 1 tablespoon butter in small skillet over medium heat; add banana slices, and cook 3 minutes or until thoroughly heated. Stir in toasted black walnuts and ¼ cup honey, and remove from heat.
3. Whisk together eggs and next 3 ingredients in a shallow dish or pie plate. Lightly press bread slices, 1 at a time, into egg mixture, coating both sides of bread. Cook bread, in batches, on a nonstick griddle coated with cooking spray over medium heat 1 to 2 minutes on each side or until done. Repeat procedure, if necessary. Transfer to a serving plate. Serve with banana mixture and syrup. **Yield**: 4 servings.

Caramel-Nut Pull-Apart Bread

prep: 12 min. • bake: 30 min.

Gooey pull-apart bread goes over well at any breakfast table. This version is a surefire wake-up call!

1   cup plus 2 tablespoons firmly packed brown sugar
1   cup chopped walnuts

¾   cup butter, melted
3   (12-ounce) cans refrigerated biscuits
2   tablespoons cinnamon sugar

1. Preheat oven to 350°. Combine brown sugar and walnuts in a small bowl. Stir in butter. Spoon half of brown sugar mixture in bottom of a greased 12-cup Bundt pan.
2. Cut each biscuit in half (use kitchen scissors for quick cutting), and place in a large bowl. Sprinkle biscuits with cinnamon sugar; toss well to coat. Arrange half of biscuits over brown sugar mixture in Bundt pan. Spoon remaining brown sugar mixture over biscuits in pan; top with remaining biscuits.
3. Bake at 350° for 30 to 35 minutes or until browned. Turn out onto a serving platter immediately, spooning any remaining sauce over bread. Serve warm. **Yield:** 12 servings.

Generations of Southern cooks have passed down the recipe for this **sticky treat.** The kid-friendly comfort food will fill your house with the welcoming aroma of cinnamon and butter.

Cacao and Milk Chocolate Scones

prep: 12 min. • bake: 18 min.

This recipe is like a sweet version of drop biscuits. Find cacao nibs packaged at gourmet food stores.

3 cups all-purpose flour
⅔ cup granulated sugar
1 tablespoon baking powder
½ teaspoon salt
¾ cup cold unsalted butter, cut into pieces
1 cup milk chocolate morsels or chopped milk chocolate bar

½ cup cacao nibs or chopped toasted pecans
1 large egg
1 cup whipping cream
2 teaspoons vanilla extract
Whipping cream (optional)
Coarse or granulated sugar (optional)

1. Preheat oven to 425°. Stir together first 4 ingredients in a large bowl; cut in butter with a pastry blender or fork until crumbly. Stir in chocolate morsels and cacao nibs.
2. Whisk together egg, 1 cup whipping cream, and vanilla; add to flour mixture, stirring with a fork just until dry ingredients are moistened and mixture forms a shaggy dough. Using a ⅓-cup measuring cup, scoop dough into mounds onto parchment paper-lined baking sheets. Brush scones with additional cream, and sprinkle with sugar, if desired.
3. Bake at 425° for 18 minutes or until golden. Serve warm. **Yield:** 14 scones.

Cacao nibs are unsweetened, roasted, and crushed cacao beans. They give these scones a toasty, bittersweet flavor. Before baking, brush scones with cream; sprinkle with sugar for a crunchy finish.

Chocolate Chunk Scones

prep: 25 min. • bake: 36 min.

Serve these big chocolate wedges for breakfast or brunch with coffee, or for dessert with a dollop of whipped cream.

4	cups all-purpose flour
⅔	cup sugar
½	cup unsweetened cocoa
4	teaspoons baking powder
1½	teaspoons baking soda
1	teaspoon salt
½	teaspoon freshly grated nutmeg
¾	cup cold butter, cut up

1	(12-ounce) package semisweet chocolate chunks
1	cup coarsely chopped walnuts or pecans (optional)
1¾	cups buttermilk
1	large egg, lightly beaten
2	teaspoons vanilla extract
2	tablespoons sugar

1. Preheat oven to 350°. Whisk together first 7 ingredients in a large bowl.

2. Cut butter into flour mixture with a pastry blender or fork until crumbly. Stir in chocolate chunks and, if desired, nuts.

3. Combine buttermilk, egg, and vanilla. Pour over crumb mixture; stir just until dry ingredients are moistened.

4. Turn dough out onto a lightly floured surface, and gently knead 3 or 4 times.

5. Divide dough in half; shape each half into a ball. Pat each into a 6-inch circle on parchment paper-lined baking sheets. Cut each circle into 6 wedges using a sharp knife (do not separate wedges). Sprinkle 2 tablespoons sugar over dough.

6. Bake at 350° for 36 minutes or until a wooden pick inserted in center comes out clean. Separate into wedges. Serve warm, or remove to a wire rack to cool. Reheat scones in microwave at HIGH 20 to 25 seconds each. **Yield:** 1 dozen.

Be sure not to **overbake** your scones or they will become too dry.

Ginger Scones

prep: 20 min. • bake: 18 min.

Scottish scones are typically wedge-shaped, like these, flavored with crystallized ginger. Top the scones with sweetened whipped cream, if desired.

2¾ cups all-purpose flour	¾ cup butter, cut up
2 teaspoons baking powder	⅓ cup chopped crystallized ginger
½ teaspoon salt	1 cup milk
½ cup sugar	

1. Preheat oven to 400°. Combine first 4 ingredients in a large bowl; cut butter into flour mixture with a pastry blender or fork until crumbly. Stir in ginger. Add milk, stirring just until dry ingredients are moistened. Turn dough out onto a lightly floured surface, and knead 10 to 15 times. Pat or roll dough to ¾-inch thickness; shape into a round, and cut dough into 8 wedges. Place wedges on a lightly greased baking sheet.

2. Bake at 400° for 18 to 22 minutes or until scones are barely golden. Cool slightly on a wire rack. Serve warm. **Yield:** 8 scones.

Test Kitchen Tip

Crystallized ginger has been cooked in a sugar syrup and coated with sugar. Before you begin to chop the ginger, coat the knife blade with vegetable cooking spray to prevent the task from becoming unmanageably sticky.

Scalloped Potatoes With Ham,
page 139

easy one-dish wonders

Baked Chicken and Rice With
Black Beans

Baked Chicken and Rice With Black Beans

prep: 25 min. • bake: 10 min. • cook: 40 min.

1   (10-ounce) package yellow rice mix
1   cup chopped onion
½   cup chopped green bell pepper
½   cup chopped carrot
1   tablespoon olive oil
2   cups cubed cooked chicken

1   (15-ounce) can black beans, drained and rinsed
1   (10-ounce) can diced tomatoes and green chiles, undrained
2   cups (8 ounces) grated Monterey Jack cheese

1. Preheat oven to 350°. Prepare rice according to package directions.
2. Meanwhile, sauté onion, bell pepper, and carrot in hot oil in a medium skillet over medium heat 10 minutes or until tender.
3. Combine hot cooked rice, onion mixture, chicken, beans, diced tomatoes and chiles, and 1½ cups cheese in a large bowl. Spoon into a lightly greased 3-quart or 13- x 9-inch baking dish; sprinkle with remaining ½ cup cheese.
4. Bake, covered, at 350° for 30 minutes; uncover and bake 10 more minutes or until cheese is melted. **Yield:** 6 to 8 servings.

Poppy Seed-Chicken Casserole

prep: 12 min. • bake: 25 min. • stand: 10 min.

This timeless casserole might just be what put poppy seeds on the map. We gave this version a healthy spin with whole wheat crackers.

3   to 4 cups chopped cooked chicken or turkey
1   (10¾-ounce) can cream of chicken and mushroom soup
1   (16-ounce) container sour cream or light sour cream

1½   cups (6 ounces) shredded sharp Cheddar cheese
3   tablespoons poppy seeds
1   sleeve whole wheat round buttery crackers, crushed
¼   cup butter, melted

1. Preheat oven to 350°. Combine first 5 ingredients in a large bowl; stir well. Spoon into a lightly greased 11- x 7-inch baking dish. Top with crushed crackers. Drizzle with melted butter.
2. Bake, uncovered, at 350° for 25 to 30 minutes or until bubbly. Let stand 10 minutes before serving. **Yield:** 6 servings.

Note: You can crush the crackers while they're still in the sleeve. Gently crush with your hands; then open crackers at one end, and sprinkle right onto the casserole.

Chicken Tetrazzini

prep: 20 min. • bake: 35 min.

Tetrazzini is a house-favorite cheese-and-chicken entrée. This version serves plenty.

1 (16-ounce) package vermicelli
½ cup chicken broth
4 cups chopped cooked chicken
1 (10¾-ounce) can cream of mushroom soup
1 (10¾-ounce) can cream of chicken soup
1 (10¾-ounce) can cream of celery soup
1 (8-ounce) container sour cream

1 (6-ounce) jar sliced mushrooms, drained
½ cup (2 ounces) shredded Parmesan cheese
1 teaspoon pepper
½ teaspoon salt
2 cups (8 ounces) shredded Cheddar cheese

freezable • make ahead • portable

1. Cook vermicelli according to package directions; drain. Return to pot, and toss with chicken broth.

2. Preheat oven to 350°. Stir together chopped cooked chicken and next 8 ingredients in a large bowl; add vermicelli, and toss well. Spoon chicken mixture into 2 lightly greased 11- x 7-inch baking dishes. Sprinkle with Cheddar cheese.

3. Bake, covered, at 350° for 30 minutes; uncover and bake 5 more minutes or until cheese is bubbly. **Yield:** 12 servings.

Note: Freeze unbaked casserole up to 1 month, if desired. Thaw casserole overnight in refrigerator. Let stand 30 minutes at room temperature, and bake as directed.

"This speedy **Italian** classic can be made ahead for an easy—and delicious—weeknight dinner."

Chicken-and-Rice Casserole

prep: 20 min. • bake: 20 min.

Use a rotisserie chicken for this family-friendly casserole. The potato chip topping promises to be a hit.

make ahead • portable

2 tablespoons butter
1 medium onion, chopped
1 (8.8-ounce) package microwaveable rice of choice
3 cups chopped cooked chicken
1½ cups frozen petite peas
1½ cups (6 ounces) shredded sharp Cheddar cheese

1 cup mayonnaise
1 (10¾-ounce) can cream of chicken soup
1 (8-ounce) can sliced water chestnuts, drained
1 (4-ounce) jar sliced pimientos, drained
3 cups coarsely crushed ridged potato chips

1. Preheat oven to 350°. Melt butter in a skillet over medium heat. Add onion, and sauté 5 minutes or until tender.

2. Cook rice in microwave according to package directions. Combine sautéed onion, rice, chicken, and next 6 ingredients in a large bowl; toss gently. Spoon mixture into a lightly greased 13- x 9-inch baking dish. Top with coarsely crushed potato chips.

3. Bake, uncovered, at 350° for 20 to 25 minutes or until bubbly. **Yield:** 8 servings.

Note: To make casserole ahead, prepare and spoon casserole into baking dish, leaving off crushed chips. Cover and refrigerate up to 24 hours. Uncover and add crushed chips before baking.

"If you use a **rotisserie chicken** for this recipe, note that a 2-pound chicken provides 3 cups of chicken."

Leslie's Favorite Chicken-and-Wild Rice Casserole

prep: 30 min. • cook: 10 min. • bake: 40 min.

This is one of those creamy, cheesy chicken casseroles. Perfect for a big family get-together, it feeds a crowd. You can make and freeze the casserole ahead, or make two smaller casseroles.

make ahead • portable • freezable

2 (6.2-ounce) packages fast-cooking long-grain and wild rice mix
¼ cup butter
4 celery ribs, chopped
2 medium onions, chopped
2 (8-ounce) cans sliced water chestnuts, drained
5 cups chopped cooked chicken
4 cups (16 ounces) shredded Cheddar cheese, divided

2 (10¾-ounce) cans cream of mushroom soup
2 (8-ounce) containers sour cream
1 cup milk
½ teaspoon salt
½ teaspoon pepper
2 cups soft, fresh breadcrumbs
1 (2.25-ounce) package sliced almonds, toasted

1. Preheat oven to 350°. Prepare rice mixes according to package directions.

2. Melt butter in a large skillet over medium heat; add celery and onions. Sauté 10 minutes or until tender. Stir in rice, water chestnuts, chicken, 3 cups cheese, and next 5 ingredients.

3. Spoon mixture into a lightly greased 4-quart baking dish or lasagna pan. Top casserole with breadcrumbs.

4. Bake at 350° for 35 minutes. Sprinkle with remaining 1 cup cheese and almonds; bake 5 more minutes. **Yield:** 10 to 12 servings.

Note: You can divide this casserole between 2 (13- x 9-inch) baking dishes. They'll just be slightly shallow as opposed to brimming over. Bake as directed above, or freeze casseroles up to 1 month. Remove from freezer, and let stand at room temperature 1 hour. Bake, covered, at 350° for 30 minutes. Uncover casseroles, and bake 55 more minutes. Sprinkle with remaining 1 cup cheese and almonds, and bake 5 more minutes.

Sausage-and-Chicken Cassoulet

prep: 25 min. • cook: 18 min. • bake: 30 min. • stand: 10 min.

A cassoulet is a French dish of beans, sausages, and meat that is covered and slowly cooked. Our Test Kitchens' version is covered with a cornbread crust.

1   (16-ounce) package smoked sausage, sliced
1   pound skinned and boned chicken breasts, chopped
1   (15.8-ounce) can great Northern beans, drained and rinsed
1   (14.5-ounce) can diced tomatoes with onion and garlic, drained
1   (14-ounce) can chicken broth
1½ teaspoons dried thyme
1   (6-ounce) package buttermilk cornbread mix
⅔   cup water or milk

1. Preheat oven to 400°. Cook sausage in a 2¼- to 3-quart ovenproof skillet over medium heat 8 minutes or until browned. Remove sausage from skillet, and drain on paper towels, reserving drippings in skillet. Set sausage aside.

2. Cook chicken in hot drippings in skillet over medium-high heat 5 minutes or until browned.

3. Return sausage to skillet with chicken. Stir in beans and next 3 ingredients. Bring to a boil.

4. Stir together cornbread mix and ⅔ cup water or milk. Pour over hot sausage mixture in skillet.

5. Bake at 400° for 30 to 35 minutes or until golden. Let stand 10 minutes before serving. **Yield:** 6 servings.

Test Kitchen Tip

Check your cookware information to make sure your skillet's handle is ovenproof up to 400° or higher. If not, just prep in a traditional skillet and then bake in a casserole dish that holds 2¼ to 3 quarts. (You can measure your dish capacity using water if the dish is not labeled.) We used a Le Creuset 2¼-quart (8½-inch-diameter x 3-inch-deep) Saucier Pan at one testing and a hand-me-down 3-quart (10-inch-diameter x 3-inch-deep) cast-iron skillet at another testing. Both skillets worked fine.

Quick-and-Easy King Ranch Chicken Casserole

prep: 30 min. • cook: 16 min. • bake: 55 min. • stand: 10 min.

- 2 tablespoons butter
- 1 medium onion, chopped
- 1 medium-size green bell pepper, chopped
- 1 garlic clove, pressed
- ¾ cup chicken broth
- 1 (10¾-ounce) can cream of mushroom soup
- 1 (10¾-ounce) can cream of chicken soup
- 2 (10-ounce) cans diced tomatoes and green chiles, drained
- 1 teaspoon dried oregano
- 1 teaspoon ground cumin
- 1 teaspoon Mexican-style or other chili powder
- 1 (2-pound) skinned, boned, and shredded deli-roasted chicken
- 3 cups (12 ounces) shredded sharp Cheddar cheese
- 3 cups coarsely crumbled lime-flavored white corn tortilla chips

make ahead • portable

1. Preheat oven to 350°. Melt butter in a large skillet over medium-high heat. Add onion, and sauté 5 minutes or until tender. Add bell pepper and garlic, and sauté 3 to 4 minutes. Stir in chicken broth, cream of mushroom soup, and next 5 ingredients. Cook, stirring occasionally, 8 minutes.
2. Layer half of shredded chicken in a lightly greased 13- x 9-inch baking dish. Top with half of soup mixture and 1 cup Cheddar cheese. Cover with half of crumbled tortilla chips. Repeat layers once. Top with remaining 1 cup cheese.
3. Bake at 350° for 55 minutes or until bubbly. Let stand 10 minutes before serving. **Yield:** 8 to 10 servings.

Creole Jambalaya

prep: 25 min. • cook: 1 hr.

Jambalaya is traditionally made in one pot, with meat, veggies, and finally rice added near the end of cooking. This Creole version, which is also referred to as Red Jambalaya, sports a tomato base. On the other hand, Cajun Jambalaya is brown, made with stock and seasonings, and has no tomato products. Preferences aside, this historic entrée remains a notable stick-to-your-ribs comfort dish.

2 tablespoons butter
1 large onion, chopped
1 green bell pepper, chopped
8 green onions, chopped
2 celery ribs, chopped
3 cups cubed cooked ham (1 pound)
1 pound Cajun-flavored or smoked sausage, sliced

1 (8-ounce) can tomato sauce
½ teaspoon salt
½ teaspoon ground black pepper
¼ teaspoon ground red pepper
5 cups cooked rice

1. Melt butter in a large skillet over medium heat. Add onion and next 3 ingredients; sauté until tender. Add ham, sausage, and next 4 ingredients. Cook, stirring occasionally, 20 minutes.
2. Stir in rice; cover and cook, stirring occasionally, 30 minutes over low heat. **Yield:** 8 servings.

"Jambalaya **leftovers** are always welcome. Store them in an airtight container in the refrigerator for up to 2 days."

Onion-Topped Sausage 'n' Mashed Potato Casserole

prep: 15 min. • cook: 11 min. • bake: 40 min. • stand: 5 min.

1   (19.5-ounce) package sweet ground turkey sausage, casings removed*

2   (14.5-ounce) cans diced tomatoes in sauce

¼   cup loosely packed fresh basil leaves, chopped**

1   shallot, chopped

1   teaspoon salt-free garlic-and-herb seasoning

1   (24-ounce) package refrigerated garlic-flavored mashed potatoes

1   (8-ounce) package shredded Italian five-cheese blend

¼   teaspoon dried Italian seasoning

1   cup French fried onions

1. Preheat oven to 350°. Brown sausage in a large skillet over medium-high heat, stirring often, 6 to 8 minutes or until meat crumbles and is no longer pink; drain.

2. Stir in tomatoes and next 3 ingredients, and cook, stirring occasionally, 5 minutes. Transfer sausage mixture to a lightly greased 11- x 7-inch baking dish.

3. Stir together mashed potatoes, cheese, and Italian seasoning in a large bowl. (Mixture will be dry.) Spread potato mixture over sausage mixture in baking dish.

4. Bake at 350° for 35 to 40 minutes or until bubbly. Top with fried onions, and bake 5 more minutes. Let stand 5 minutes before serving. **Yield:** 6 servings.

*1 (1¼-pound) package ground chicken sausage may be substituted.
**½ teaspoon dried basil may be substituted.

Scalloped Potatoes With Ham

prep: 20 min. • bake: 1 hr., 10 min. • stand: 10 min.

Nutty Gruyère cheese and sweet potatoes give this dish fresh appeal.

1	medium onion, chopped	1	teaspoon salt
1	tablespoon vegetable oil	¼	teaspoon pepper
3	garlic cloves, finely chopped	2	cups chopped cooked ham
2	sweet potatoes, peeled and cut into ¼-inch slices (about 1½ pounds)	2	cups (8 ounces) shredded Gruyère cheese, divided
2	baking potatoes, peeled and cut into ¼-inch slices (about 1½ pounds)	1¾	cups whipping cream
½	cup all-purpose flour	2	tablespoons butter, cut into pieces

1. Sauté onion in oil over medium-high heat 5 minutes or until tender. Add garlic; cook 30 seconds. Remove from heat, and set aside. Place potatoes in a large bowl.

2. Preheat oven to 400°. Combine flour, salt, and pepper; sprinkle over potatoes, tossing to coat. Arrange half of potato mixture in a greased 13- x 9-inch baking dish or 3-quart gratin dish. Top with onion, ham, and 1 cup cheese. Top with remaining potato mixture. Pour cream over potato mixture. Dot with butter, and cover with aluminum foil.

3. Bake at 400° for 50 minutes. Uncover, top with remaining 1 cup cheese, and bake 20 more minutes or until potatoes are tender and cheese is browned. Let stand 10 minutes before serving. **Yield:** 6 servings.

The **Gruyère cheese** and **whipping cream** make this one-dish meal extra rich and creamy.

Fabulous Tuna-Noodle Casserole

prep: 18 min. • cook: 15 min. • bake: 40 min.

¼ cup butter
1 large red bell pepper, chopped
1 cup chopped onion
1 (8-ounce) package sliced fresh mushrooms
⅓ cup all-purpose flour
3 cups milk
3 cups (12 ounces) shredded Cheddar cheese
¾ teaspoon salt

½ teaspoon pepper
1 (12-ounce) can solid white tuna in spring water, drained and flaked
1 (6-ounce) can solid white tuna in spring water, drained and flaked
1 (12-ounce) package egg noodles, cooked
¼ cup chopped fresh flat-leaf parsley
1½ cups soft, fresh breadcrumbs
⅓ cup butter, melted

1. Preheat oven to 375°. Melt ¼ cup butter in a large skillet over medium-high heat; add bell pepper, onion, and mushrooms, and sauté 5 minutes or until tender. Remove from skillet.
2. Whisk together flour and milk until smooth; add to skillet. Cook over medium heat, stirring constantly, 10 minutes or until thickened. Remove from heat; add cheese, salt, and pepper, stirring until cheese is melted.
3. Stir in tuna, noodles, and parsley; stir in sautéed vegetables. Spoon into a lightly greased 13- x 9-inch baking dish.
4. Bake, covered, at 375° for 25 minutes. Stir together breadcrumbs and ⅓ cup melted butter; sprinkle over casserole, and bake, uncovered, 15 more minutes or until golden.
Yield: 6 to 8 servings.

> Fresh veggies and a **cheesy, rich** sauce make this one of the best tuna casseroles that we've tried.

Shrimp Casserole

prep: 30 min. • cook: 17 min. • bake: 25 min.

1½ cups uncooked long-grain rice	4 green onions, chopped
1½ pounds medium-size raw shrimp	2 (10¾-ounce) cans cream of shrimp soup*
½ cup butter	¼ teaspoon salt
1 green bell pepper, chopped	¼ teaspoon freshly ground black pepper
1 onion, chopped	1 cup (4 ounces) shredded Cheddar-colby cheese blend
3 celery ribs, chopped	
2 garlic cloves, minced	¼ cup fine, dry breadcrumbs

1. Preheat oven to 350°. Prepare rice according to package directions.

2. Peel shrimp, and devein, if desired.

3. Melt butter in a large skillet over medium heat; add bell pepper and next 4 ingredients, and sauté 10 to 12 minutes or until tender. Stir in soup, shrimp, salt, and black pepper; cook 3 minutes or just until shrimp turn pink. (Do not overcook.)

4. Combine shrimp mixture and rice. Pour mixture into a lightly greased 13- x 9-inch baking dish. Sprinkle with 1 cup shredded cheese and ¼ cup breadcrumbs.

5. Bake at 350° for 25 minutes or until cheese is melted. **Yield:** 8 servings.

*2 (10¾-ounce) cans cream of celery soup may be substituted.

Variation

Chicken Casserole: Substitute 3 cups chopped cooked chicken for shrimp and 2 (10¾-ounce) cans cream of chicken soup for cream of shrimp soup. Proceed with recipe as directed.

Spinach-Ravioli Lasagna

Spinach-Ravioli Lasagna

prep: 10 min. • bake: 35 min.

- 1 (6-ounce) package fresh baby spinach
- ⅓ cup pesto sauce
- 1 (15-ounce) jar Alfredo sauce
- ¼ cup vegetable broth
- 1 (25-ounce) package frozen cheese-filled ravioli (do not thaw)
- 1 cup (4 ounces) shredded Italian six-cheese blend

Garnishes: chopped fresh basil, paprika

1. Preheat oven to 375°. Chop spinach, and toss with pesto in a medium bowl.

2. Combine Alfredo sauce and vegetable broth. Spoon one-third of Alfredo sauce mixture (about ½ cup) into a lightly greased 2.2-quart or 11- x 7-inch baking dish. Top with half of spinach mixture. Arrange half of ravioli in a single layer over spinach mixture. Repeat layers once. Top with remaining Alfredo sauce.

3. Bake at 375° for 30 minutes. Remove from oven, and sprinkle with shredded cheese. Bake 5 more minutes or until hot and bubbly. Garnish, if desired. **Yield:** 6 to 8 servings.

Four-Cheese Macaroni

prep: 40 min. • cook: 41 min.

- 12 ounces uncooked cavatappi
- ½ cup butter
- ½ cup all-purpose flour
- ½ teaspoon ground red pepper
- 3 cups milk
- 2 cups (8 ounces) freshly shredded white Cheddar cheese
- 1 cup (4 ounces) freshly shredded Monterey Jack cheese
- 1 cup (4 ounces) freshly shredded fontina cheese
- 1 cup (4 ounces) freshly shredded Asiago cheese
- 1½ cups soft, fresh breadcrumbs
- ½ cup chopped cooked bacon
- 2 tablespoons butter, melted

1. Preheat oven to 350°. Prepare pasta according to package directions.

2. Meanwhile, melt ½ cup butter in a Dutch oven over low heat. Whisk in flour and ground red pepper until smooth; cook, whisking constantly, 1 minute. Gradually whisk in milk; cook over medium heat, whisking constantly, 6 to 7 minutes or until thickened. Remove from heat.

3. Toss together Cheddar cheese and next 3 ingredients in a medium bowl; reserve 1½ cups cheese mixture. Add remaining cheese mixture and hot cooked pasta to sauce, tossing to coat. Pour into a lightly greased 13- x 9-inch baking dish or 12-inch cast-iron skillet. Top with reserved 1½ cups cheese mixture.

4. Toss together breadcrumbs and next 2 ingredients; sprinkle over cheese mixture.

5. Bake, uncovered, at 350° for 35 to 40 minutes or until golden and bubbly. **Yield:** 8 servings.

Saucy Manicotti

prep: 30 min. • cook: 10 min. • bake: 50 min.

Crusty cheese bubbling over gratin dishes and blanketing a thick meat sauce will please anyone at your dinner table.

1 (8-ounce) package manicotti shells
1 (16-ounce) package Italian sausage, casings removed
1 large onion, chopped
9 garlic cloves, pressed and divided
1 (26-ounce) jar seven-herb tomato pasta sauce

1 (8-ounce) container chive-and-onion cream cheese
6 cups (24 ounces) shredded mozzarella cheese, divided
¾ cup freshly grated Parmesan cheese
1 (15-ounce) container ricotta cheese
¾ teaspoon freshly ground pepper

1. Cook manicotti shells according to package directions, and drain.

2. Cook sausage, onion, and half of pressed garlic in a large Dutch oven over medium-high heat 6 minutes, stirring until sausage crumbles and is no longer pink. Stir in pasta sauce; bring to a boil. Remove from heat.

3. Preheat oven to 350°. Combine cream cheese, 4 cups mozzarella cheese, next 3 ingredients, and remaining pressed garlic in a large bowl, stirring until blended. Cut a slit down length of each cooked manicotti shell.

4. Spoon 1 cup sauce mixture into a lightly greased 13- x 9-inch baking dish. Spoon cheese mixture into manicotti shells, gently pressing cut sides together. Arrange stuffed shells over sauce in dish, seam sides down. Spoon remaining sauce over stuffed shells. Sprinkle with remaining 2 cups mozzarella cheese.

5. Bake, covered, at 350° for 50 minutes or until bubbly. **Yield:** 7 servings.

Note: For individual casseroles, spoon ¼ cup sauce into each of 7 lightly greased 8-ounce shallow baking dishes. Top each with 2 filled manicotti shells. Top with remaining sauce (about ¾ cup per dish) and remaining mozzarella cheese. Bake, uncovered, at 350° for 50 minutes.

Chicken Lasagna With Roasted Red Bell Pepper Sauce

prep: 20 min. • bake: 1 hr., 5 min.

A pan of hot, bubbly lasagna is pure bliss on a cold winter's night, especially when paired with a robust red wine.

4 cups finely chopped cooked chicken
2 (8-ounce) containers chive-and-onion cream cheese
1 (10-ounce) package frozen chopped spinach, thawed and well drained
1 teaspoon seasoned pepper

¾ teaspoon garlic salt
Roasted Red Bell Pepper Sauce
9 no-boil lasagna noodles
2 cups (8 ounces) shredded Italian three-cheese blend

1. Preheat oven to 350°. Stir together first 5 ingredients.
2. Layer a lightly greased 11- x 7-inch baking dish with one-third of Roasted Red Bell Pepper Sauce, 3 noodles, one-third of chicken mixture, and one-third of cheese. Repeat layers twice. Place baking dish on a baking sheet.
3. Bake, covered, at 350° for 50 to 55 minutes or until thoroughly heated. Uncover and bake 15 more minutes. **Yield:** 6 to 8 servings.

Roasted Red Bell Pepper Sauce

prep: 5 min.

This sauce is also great over your favorite noodles.

1 (12-ounce) jar roasted red bell peppers, drained
1 (16-ounce) jar creamy Alfredo sauce

1 (3-ounce) package shredded Parmesan cheese
½ teaspoon dried crushed red pepper

1. Process all ingredients in a food processor until smooth, stopping to scrape down sides. **Yield:** 3½ cups.

Ultimate Nachos

prep: 13 min. • cook: 5 min. • bake: 8 min.

⅓ cup finely chopped onion
1 large garlic clove, minced
1 tablespoon olive oil
1 (16-ounce) can refried beans
½ cup fresh salsa
1 (13-ounce) package restaurant-style tortilla chips
1½ cups (6 ounces) shredded Monterey Jack cheese

1½ cups (6 ounces) shredded Cheddar cheese
Pickled jalapeño slices, well drained
1 cup guacamole (optional)
½ cup sour cream (optional)
Toppings: chopped fresh cilantro, sliced ripe olives, shredded lettuce, additional fresh salsa

1. Preheat oven to 450°. Sauté onion and garlic in hot oil in a skillet over medium heat 4 to 5 minutes or until onion is tender. Add beans and salsa to pan, stirring until beans are creamy. Cook 1 minute or until heated.
2. Scatter most of chips on a parchment paper-lined large baking sheet or an ovenproof platter. Top with bean mixture, cheeses, and desired amount of jalapeños.
3. Bake at 450° for 8 minutes or until cheese melts and edges are lightly browned.
4. Top with small dollops of guacamole and sour cream, if desired. Add desired toppings. Serve hot. **Yield:** 6 servings.

Taco Casserole

prep: 10 min. • cook: 10 min. • bake: 25 min.

Certainly tacos qualify as timeless comfort food. This dish makes use of all the familiar elements and then gets a nacho chip topping. Serve it with a lettuce wedge salad, and you've got a meal.

1 pound ground chuck
½ cup chopped onion
1 (1.25-ounce) package taco seasoning mix
1 (16-ounce) can chili beans, undrained
1 (8-ounce) can tomato sauce

2 cups (8 ounces) shredded colby cheese
5 cups coarsely crushed nacho cheese-flavored tortilla chips or other flavor tortilla chips (about 9 ounces)

1. Preheat oven to 350°. Brown ground chuck with onion in a large skillet over medium heat. Stir until beef crumbles and onion is tender; drain.

2. Return beef mixture to skillet; stir in taco seasoning, beans, and tomato sauce. Layer half each of beef mixture, shredded cheese, and tortilla chips in a lightly greased 13- x 9-inch baking dish. Repeat procedure with remaining beef mixture, shredded cheese, and tortilla chips.

3. Bake, uncovered, at 350° for 25 minutes or until casserole is thoroughly heated. **Yield:** 6 servings.

"This easy recipe offers appealing **texture** and **bold flavor** for a great family meal."

Homestyle Ground Beef Casserole

prep: 8 min. • cook: 15 min. • bake: 40 min. • stand: 10 min.

Hamburger casserole works for any weeknight and is a universal family favorite. Green beans and corn would round out the plate nicely.

1 pound ground round
1 (14½-ounce) can diced tomatoes with basil, garlic, and oregano, undrained
1 (10-ounce) can diced tomatoes and green chiles, undrained
1 (6-ounce) can tomato paste
1 teaspoon salt
½ teaspoon dried Italian seasoning
¼ teaspoon pepper
3 cups uncooked medium egg noodles

5 green onions, chopped
1 (8-ounce) container sour cream
1 (3-ounce) package cream cheese, softened
1 cup (4 ounces) shredded sharp Cheddar cheese
1 cup (4 ounces) shredded Parmesan cheese
1 cup (4 ounces) shredded mozzarella cheese

1. Cook ground round in a large skillet over medium heat 8 minutes, stirring until it crumbles and is no longer pink. Stir in both cans diced tomatoes and next 4 ingredients. Bring to a boil; reduce heat, and simmer, uncovered, 5 minutes. Remove from heat; set aside.

2. Preheat oven to 350°. Cook egg noodles in boiling salted water according to package directions; drain. Stir together hot cooked noodles, chopped green onions, sour cream, and cream cheese until blended.

3. Spoon egg noodles into a lightly greased 13- x 9-inch or other similar-size baking dish. Top with beef mixture; sprinkle with shredded cheeses in the order listed.

4. Bake, covered, at 350° for 35 minutes. Uncover and bake 5 more minutes. Let stand 10 to 15 minutes before serving. **Yield:** 6 servings.

Note: Freeze assembled, unbaked casserole up to 1 month, if desired. Thaw in refrigerator overnight. Bake as directed.

Baked Four-Cheese Spaghetti With Italian Sausage

prep: 15 min. • cook: 3 hr., 5 min. • stand: 10 min.

8 ounces uncooked spaghetti

1 pound Italian sausage (about 4 links)

1 (8-ounce) container refrigerated prechopped bell pepper-and-onion mix

2 teaspoons jarred minced garlic

1 tablespoon vegetable oil

1 (24-ounce) jar fire-roasted tomato and garlic pasta sauce

1 (16-ounce) package shredded sharp Cheddar cheese

1 (8-ounce) package shredded mozzarella cheese

4 ounces fontina cheese, shredded

½ cup (2 ounces) preshredded Parmesan cheese

1. Cook pasta in boiling salted water in a large Dutch oven according to package directions. Drain and return to pan.

2. Meanwhile, brown sausage, bell pepper mix, and garlic in oil in a large nonstick skillet over medium-high heat, stirring often, 8 to 10 minutes or until meat crumbles and is no longer pink. Drain. Stir meat mixture, pasta sauce, and Cheddar cheese into pasta. Spoon half of pasta mixture into a lightly greased 5-quart slow cooker coated with cooking spray.

3. Combine mozzarella cheese and fontina cheese. Sprinkle half of mozzarella mixture over pasta mixture in slow cooker. Top with remaining pasta mixture, remaining mozzarella mixture, and Parmesan cheese. Cover and cook on LOW 3 hours. Let stand, covered, 10 minutes before serving. **Yield:** 8 to 10 servings.

Chalupa Dinner Bowl

prep: 30 min. • cook: 7 hr.

This pork-and-bean mixture is versatile. Serve it spooned over cornbread or rolled up burrito-style in flour tortillas. Make hearty nachos, quesadillas, or tacos with it, too. It can even be used as a meaty addition to huevos rancheros (fried corn tortillas topped with fried eggs and salsa).

1 pound dried pinto beans
1 (3½-pound) bone-in pork loin roast
2 (4-ounce) cans chopped green chiles
2 garlic cloves, chopped
1 tablespoon chili powder
2 teaspoons salt
1 teaspoon dried oregano
1 teaspoon ground cumin
1 (32-ounce) container chicken broth
1 (10-ounce) can diced tomatoes and green chiles with lime juice and cilantro
8 taco salad shells
1 small head iceberg lettuce, shredded
Toppings: shredded Monterey Jack cheese, pickled jalapeño pepper slices, halved grape tomatoes, sour cream, sliced avocado

1. Rinse and sort beans according to package directions.

2. Place pinto beans in a 6-quart slow cooker; add roast and next 6 ingredients. Pour chicken broth over top of roast.

3. Cover and cook on HIGH 1 hour; reduce heat to LOW, and cook 9 hours. Or, cover and cook on HIGH 6 hours. Remove bones and fat from roast; pull roast into large pieces with 2 forks. Stir in diced tomatoes and green chiles. Cook, uncovered, on HIGH 1 more hour or until liquid is slightly thickened.

4. Heat taco salad shells according to package directions; place shredded lettuce into shells. Spoon about 1 cup pork-and-bean mixture into each shell using a slotted spoon. Serve with desired toppings. **Yield:** 8 servings.

Chicken Enchilada Dip

prep: 10 min. • cook: 4 hr.

The corn tortillas cook into this dish and thicken it—you won't see them after they're cooked, but you'll taste their authentic Mexican flavor.

make ahead • portable

2 (10-ounce) cans mild green chile enchilada sauce
10 (6-inch) corn tortillas, torn into 3-inch pieces
4 cups pulled cooked chicken breasts
1½ cups sour cream
1 (12-ounce) package shredded colby-Jack cheese blend

1 (10¾-ounce) can cream of mushroom soup
8 cups shredded iceberg lettuce
1 (15-ounce) can black beans, drained and rinsed
3 tomatoes, diced
Tortilla chips

1. Spoon ½ cup enchilada sauce over bottom of a greased 4-quart slow cooker. Add enough tortilla pieces to cover sauce.

2. Stir together chicken, sour cream, 2 cups cheese, and soup. Spread 2 cups chicken mixture over tortilla pieces. Top with tortilla pieces to cover. Drizzle with ½ cup enchilada sauce. Repeat layers twice, ending with tortilla pieces and remaining enchilada sauce. Sprinkle with remaining 1 cup cheese.

3. Cover and cook on LOW 4 hours. Place lettuce on plates; top with chicken, beans, and tomatoes. Serve hot. Serve with tortilla chips. **Yield:** 8 servings.

To find the tastiest **fresh tomatoes,** smell them; a good tomato should smell like a tomato, especially at the stem end.

Sesame Chicken

prep: 7 min. • cook: 2 hr., 30 min.

1¼ cups chicken broth
½ cup firmly packed brown sugar
¼ cup cornstarch
2 tablespoons rice vinegar
2 tablespoons soy sauce
2 tablespoons sweet chili sauce
2 tablespoons honey
2 teaspoons dark sesame oil

1½ pounds skinned and boned chicken breasts, cut into 1-inch pieces
2 cups sugar snap peas
2 cups crinkle-cut carrots
1½ tablespoons sesame seeds, toasted
Hot cooked rice
Garnish: chopped green onions

1. Whisk together first 8 ingredients in a 4-quart slow cooker. Stir in chicken. Cover and cook on HIGH 2½ hours or until chicken is done, stirring after 1½ hours.

2. Steam sugar snap peas and carrots. Stir vegetable mixture and sesame seeds into slow cooker. Serve over hot cooked rice. Garnish, if desired. **Yield:** 4 to 6 servings.

> Lifting the lid on a **slow cooker** releases a great deal of heat so purchase one with a **clear lid.**

Seafood Pot Pie

prep: 15 min. • cook: 3 hr.

Parchment paper

¼ cup butter

1 cup chopped onion or 1 leek, thinly sliced

2 teaspoons jarred minced garlic

1 (8-ounce) package sliced baby portobello mushrooms

¼ cup all-purpose flour

1 cup half-and-half

1 cup chicken broth

1 (11-ounce) package frozen baby broccoli blend

1 (1-pound) cod fillet, cut into 2-inch pieces

½ pound fresh lump crabmeat, drained and picked free of shell

½ teaspoon salt

½ teaspoon freshly ground pepper

½ (17.3-ounce) package frozen puff pastry sheets, thawed

1 egg yolk, beaten

¼ cup dry sherry

1. To make a template for pastry lid, place a 3½-quart slow-cooker lid on parchment paper; trace lid shape. Remove lid. Cut out parchment-paper shape, and set aside.

2. Melt butter in a large skillet over medium-high heat. Add onion, garlic, and mushrooms; sauté 5 minutes. Whisk in flour until smooth. Cook 1 minute, whisking constantly. Gradually whisk in half-and-half and broth; cook over medium heat, whisking constantly, until thickened and bubbly. Transfer to a slow cooker. Stir in vegetables. Cover and cook on LOW 2 hours. Uncover and stir in cod, crabmeat, salt, and pepper. (Cooker will be almost full.) Cover and cook on HIGH 1 hour or until cod flakes with a fork.

3. Preheat oven to 400°. Roll out 1 pastry sheet on a lightly floured surface until smooth. Place parchment template on pastry, and cut out pastry using a paring knife. Place pastry on a parchment paper-lined baking sheet. Brush with egg yolk. Bake at 400° for 14 to 15 minutes. Stir sherry into pot pie mixture. Spoon onto serving plates. Top pot pie mixture with pastry lid just before serving. Serve hot. **Yield:** 6 servings.

Lowcountry Boil

prep: 4 min. • cook: 5 hr.,15 min. • stand: 15 min.

make ahead

12 small new potatoes (1¼ pounds)
1 (12-ounce) can beer
4 to 5 tablespoons Old Bay seasoning
2 celery ribs, cut into 4-inch pieces
1 onion, quartered
2 lemons, halved

1 pound kielbasa sausage, cut into 1-inch pieces
½ (12-count) package frozen corn on the cob (do not thaw)
2 pounds unpeeled, large raw shrimp
Cocktail sauce

1. Place potatoes in a 7-quart slow cooker. Add 10 cups water, beer, and next 3 ingredients. Squeeze juice from lemon halves into mixture in slow cooker; add lemon halves to slow cooker. Cover and cook on LOW 3 hours.

2. Add sausage and corn. Cover and cook on LOW 2 hours. Add shrimp; stir gently. Cover and cook on HIGH 15 minutes or until shrimp turn pink. Turn off cooker; let stand 15 minutes. Drain. Serve with cocktail sauce. **Yield:** 6 servings.

"This is an easy **dump-and-go** recipe. Just pay attention to the times for adding the different ingredients."

Beef-and-Vegetable Stir-Fry

Beef-and-Vegetable Stir-Fry

prep: 25 min. • cook: 10 min.

1 pound fresh asparagus
12 ounces top round steak, cut into thin strips
3 tablespoons all-purpose flour
¼ cup soy sauce
2 garlic cloves, minced
1 tablespoon dark sesame oil, divided
1 tablespoon hoisin sauce

¼ teaspoon dried crushed red pepper
4 small carrots, cut diagonally into ¼-inch-thick slices
1 small red bell pepper, cut into thin strips
½ cup sliced fresh mushrooms
5 green onions, cut into 1-inch pieces
2 cups hot cooked rice

make ahead

1. Snap off tough ends of asparagus; cut spears into 1-inch pieces, and set aside.
2. Dredge steak in flour; set aside.
3. Stir together soy sauce, ¼ cup water, garlic, 1 teaspoon sesame oil, hoisin sauce, and red pepper.
4. Heat remaining 2 teaspoons oil in a large skillet or wok over medium-high heat 2 minutes. Add beef and carrot, and stir-fry 4 minutes. Add soy sauce mixture, and stir-fry 1 minute. Add asparagus, bell pepper, mushrooms, and green onions, and stir-fry 3 minutes. Serve over rice.
Yield: 4 servings.

Thai Lemon Beef

prep: 20 min. • chill: 30 min. • cook: 5 min.

1 (1-inch-thick) top round steak
⅓ cup soy sauce
¼ cup lemon juice
2 to 3 teaspoons dried crushed red pepper
4 garlic cloves, minced
1 tablespoon vegetable oil

4 green onions, cut into 2-inch pieces
2 carrots, thinly sliced
2 teaspoons cornstarch
Hot cooked ramen noodles
Garnishes: lemon zest strips, fresh basil sprigs

1. Cut steak across the grain into ⅛-inch-thick strips, and place in a medium bowl.
2. Combine soy sauce, next 3 ingredients, and ¼ cup water. Reserve half of mixture. Pour remaining half of mixture over steak. Cover and chill 30 minutes.
3. Drain steak, discarding marinade.
4. Stir-fry half of steak in ½ tablespoon hot oil in a large nonstick skillet or wok over medium-high heat 1 minute or until outside of beef is no longer pink. Remove from skillet, and repeat procedure with remaining oil and steak. Remove from skillet.
5. Add green onions and carrot to skillet, and stir-fry 3 minutes or until crisp-tender.
6. Whisk cornstarch into reserved soy sauce mixture; stir into vegetables, and stir-fry until thickened. Add steak, and stir-fry until thoroughly heated. Serve over noodles. Garnish, if desired. **Yield:** 4 servings.

Creole Fried Rice

prep: 20 min. • cook: 36 min. • cool: 30 min.

1	cup uncooked long-grain rice		½	small onion, chopped
2	cups chicken broth		½	small green bell pepper, chopped
1	pound skinned and boned chicken thighs		2	garlic cloves, chopped
1½	teaspoons Creole seasoning, divided		1	cup frozen sliced okra, thawed
2	tablespoons vegetable oil		3	plum tomatoes, chopped
½	pound andouille or smoked sausage, sliced		2	green onions, sliced (green part only)

1. Cook rice according to package directions, substituting 2 cups chicken broth for water. Spread cooked rice in a thin layer on a baking sheet. Let cool 30 minutes or until completely cool.

2. Cut chicken thighs into 1-inch pieces, and toss with 1 teaspoon Creole seasoning.

3. Cook chicken in hot oil in a large skillet over medium heat 3 minutes; add sausage, and cook 3 to 4 minutes or until lightly browned. Add onion, bell pepper, and garlic, and cook 5 minutes or until onion is tender. Stir in okra and remaining ½ teaspoon Creole seasoning. Increase heat to high; add rice, and cook, stirring constantly, 4 minutes or until thoroughly heated. Stir in tomatoes. Sprinkle with sliced green onions, and serve immediately. **Yield:** 6 servings.

Cold rice works best in this recipe. If possible, make the rice a day ahead, and store it in the fridge. If you're in a hurry, follow **Step 1** to cool it on a baking sheet.

Hot Sesame Pork on Mixed Greens

prep: 19 min. • cook: 12 min.

½	(16-ounce) package won ton wrappers
2	pounds boneless pork loin, trimmed
¾	cup sesame seeds, divided
1	cup vegetable oil, divided
½	cup all-purpose flour
1	teaspoon salt
½	teaspoon pepper
¼	cup dark sesame oil
½	cup firmly packed brown sugar
⅓	cup soy sauce
¼	cup rice vinegar
10	to 12 small green onions, sliced
2	(5-ounce) packages mixed salad greens
1	bok choy, shredded

1. Cut won ton wrappers into ½-inch strips, and cut pork into 3- x 1-inch strips; set aside.

2. Toast ½ cup sesame seeds in a large heavy skillet over medium-high heat, stirring constantly, 2 to 3 minutes; remove from skillet.

3. Pour ½ cup vegetable oil into skillet; heat to 375°. Fry won ton strips in batches until golden. Drain on paper towels; set aside. Drain skillet.

4. Combine remaining ¼ cup sesame seeds, flour, salt, and pepper in a zip-top plastic freezer bag; add pork. Seal and shake to coat.

5. Pour 2 tablespoons sesame oil into skillet; place over medium heat. Fry half of pork in hot oil, stirring often, 6 to 8 minutes or until golden. Remove and keep warm. Repeat procedure with remaining 2 tablespoons sesame oil and pork.

6. Process toasted sesame seeds, remaining ½ cup vegetable oil, ½ cup brown sugar, soy sauce, and vinegar in a blender 1 to 2 minutes or until smooth.

7. Combine pork and green onions; drizzle with soy sauce mixture, tossing gently.

8. Combine mixed greens and bok choy; top with pork mixture and fried won ton strips. Serve immediately. **Yield:** 8 servings.

Easy Skillet Tacos

prep: 10 min. • cook: 25 min. • stand: 5 min.

Tacos are an easy go-to on a busy weeknight because all you have to do is prepare the beef and chop the toppings, and everyone can make their own tacos.

1 pound ground beef
1 small onion, chopped
1 teaspoon olive oil
1 tablespoon chili powder
1½ teaspoons ground cumin
1 teaspoon salt
1 (15-ounce) can pinto beans, drained and rinsed

1 (8-ounce) can tomato sauce
½ cup salsa
1½ cups (6 ounces) shredded Cheddar cheese
1 tablespoon chopped fresh cilantro
Taco shells or flour tortillas, warmed
Toppings: shredded lettuce, diced tomatoes, salsa, sour cream

1. Cook ground beef in a large skillet over medium-high heat, stirring until beef crumbles and is no longer pink. Drain well. Remove beef; wipe skillet with a paper towel.

2. Sauté onion in hot oil in same skillet over medium-high heat. Add chili powder, cumin, salt, and beef. Cook 5 to 7 minutes, stirring occasionally. Stir in beans, tomato sauce, ¾ cup water, and salsa. Mash pinto beans in skillet with a fork, leaving some beans whole. Bring to a boil; reduce heat, and simmer, uncovered, 8 to 10 minutes or until liquid is reduced.

3. Top with cheese and cilantro. Cover, turn off heat, and let stand 5 minutes or until cheese melts. Serve with taco shells or tortillas and desired toppings. **Yield:** 4 to 6 servings.

These tacos get their flavor from **cumin** and **chili powder** without the additional sodium often found in packaged seasoning mix.

Crunchy Fried Okra,
page 195

farm-fresh favorites

Homemade Applesauce

prep: 20 min. • cook: 20 min.

For the best taste and texture, use a variety of apples—such as Granny Smith, Golden Delicious, and Gala—when making applesauce and apple pie. Stir in a little chopped rosemary, and serve this applesauce as a side dish with pork chops or hash browns.

12	large apples, peeled and coarsely chopped	1	cup sugar
		½	lemon, sliced

1. Cook all ingredients in a Dutch oven over medium heat, stirring often, 20 minutes or until apples are tender and juices are thickened. Remove and discard lemon slices. Serve applesauce warm, or let cool, and store in an airtight container in the refrigerator for up to 1 week. **Yield:** about 6 cups.

Variation

Spiced Applesauce: Substitute ½ cup firmly packed brown sugar and ½ cup granulated sugar for 1 cup sugar. Omit lemon slices, and add 1 teaspoon ground cinnamon and ¼ teaspoon ground cloves; prepare as directed.

make ahead • portable

"You can also use this **fresh favorite** to make a variety of delicious dishes such as cakes, chutneys, and pies."

Home-Style Butter Beans

prep: 10 min. • cook: 2 hr., 6 min.

5	bacon slices, diced	¼	cup butter
1	small onion, minced	2	teaspoons salt
½	cup firmly packed brown sugar	1	teaspoon cracked pepper
1	(16-ounce) package frozen butter beans		

1. Cook bacon and onion in a large Dutch oven over medium heat 5 to 7 minutes. Add brown sugar, and cook, stirring occasionally, 1 to 2 minutes or until sugar is dissolved. Stir in butter beans and butter until butter is melted and beans are thoroughly coated. Stir in 12 cups water.
2. Bring to a boil over medium-high heat; reduce heat to low, and simmer, stirring occasionally, 2 hours or until beans are very tender and liquid is thickened and just below top of beans. Stir in salt and pepper. **Yield:** 6 to 8 servings.

Variation
Home-Style Lima Beans: Substitute 1 (16-ounce) package frozen baby lima beans for butter beans. Proceed with recipe as directed.

"Cooked **beans** freeze beautifully so you can make a double batch and save some to enjoy later."

Butter Beans With Cornbread Crust

prep: 15 min. • cook: 30 min. • bake: 20 min.

As an option, look for fresh speckled butter beans late in the summer at your local farmers market. Simmer the fresh beans a few minutes less.

4	cups chicken broth		1	large sweet onion, diced
2	(16-ounce) packages frozen butter beans		1	poblano pepper, diced
½	teaspoon salt		1	tablespoon olive oil
½	teaspoon pepper			Cornbread Crust Batter

1. Bring first 4 ingredients to a boil in a large saucepan over medium-high heat. Reduce heat to low; cover and simmer 25 minutes or until beans are tender. Remove from heat.
2. Preheat oven to 425°. Sauté onion and pepper in hot oil in a large skillet over medium-high heat 2 minutes; remove from heat, and stir into beans. Spoon bean mixture into a lightly greased 13- x 9-inch baking dish.
3. Spoon Cornbread Crust Batter over beans, spreading to edges of dish.
4. Bake at 425° for 20 minutes or until crust is golden brown. **Yield:** 6 to 8 servings.

Cornbread Crust Batter

prep: 5 min.

2	cups cornmeal mix		½	cup sour cream
½	cup buttermilk		2	large eggs, lightly beaten

1. Stir together all ingredients. **Yield:** 3 cups.

Broccoli-Carrot Salad

prep: 20 min.

Variations of this old-fashioned, slightly sweet broccoli salad have made many an appearance at church suppers across the South.

1½	pounds fresh broccoli	2	to 3 tablespoons sugar
1	cup peeled, sliced, or shredded carrot	2	teaspoons red wine vinegar
1	cup (4 ounces) shredded Cheddar cheese		Lettuce leaves (optional)
1	cup raisins (optional)	8	bacon slices, cooked and crumbled
½	cup mayonnaise		

1. Remove broccoli leaves, and cut off tough ends of stalks; discard. Wash broccoli thoroughly, and cut into florets. Blanch broccoli in boiling water 10 seconds. Plunge into ice water to stop the cooking process; drain well.

2. Combine broccoli, carrot, cheese, and, if desired, raisins, tossing gently. Combine mayonnaise, sugar, and vinegar; stir well. Add mayonnaise dressing to broccoli mixture, and toss gently.

3. Spoon broccoli salad onto lettuce-lined salad plates, if desired, using a slotted spoon. Sprinkle with bacon, and serve immediately. **Yield:** 8 servings.

Fresh Corn Cakes

prep: 20 min. • cook: 5 min. per batch

Golden brown and hot off the griddle, these corn cakes are loaded with bits of melted mozzarella.

2½	cups fresh corn kernels (about 5 ears)	1	(8-ounce) package fresh mozzarella cheese, shredded
3	large eggs		
¾	cup milk	2	tablespoons chopped fresh chives
3	tablespoons butter, melted	1	teaspoon salt
¾	cup all-purpose flour	1	teaspoon freshly ground pepper
¾	cup yellow or white cornmeal		

1. Pulse first 4 ingredients in a food processor 3 or 4 times or just until corn is coarsely chopped.

2. Stir together flour and next 5 ingredients in a large bowl; stir in corn mixture just until dry ingredients are moistened.

3. Spoon ⅛ cup batter for each cake onto a hot, lightly greased griddle or large nonstick skillet to form 2-inch cakes (do not spread or flatten cakes). Cook cakes 3 to 4 minutes or until tops are covered with bubbles and edges look cooked. Turn and cook other sides 2 to 3 minutes. **Yield:** about 3 dozen.

Fried Corn

prep: 15 min. • cook: 27 min.

12	ears fresh corn	2	to 4 tablespoons sugar
8	bacon slices	2	teaspoons salt
½	cup butter	½	teaspoon pepper

1. Remove and discard husks and silks from corn. Cut off tips of corn kernels into a large bowl; scrape milk and remaining pulp from cob with a paring knife.
2. Cook bacon in a large skillet until crisp; remove bacon, reserving 3 tablespoons drippings in skillet. Crumble bacon.
3. Cook corn, butter, and next 3 ingredients in bacon drippings over medium heat 20 minutes or until corn is lightly browned, stirring often. Spoon corn into a serving dish; sprinkle with bacon. **Yield**: 12 servings.

Sweet Corn and Zucchini

Sweet Corn and Zucchini

prep: 20 min. • cook: 10 min.

2	cups coarsely chopped zucchini	2	cups fresh corn kernels
½	cup diced sweet onion	¼	cup chopped fresh chives
3	tablespoons butter	2	teaspoons taco seasoning mix

1. Sauté zucchini and onion in butter in a large skillet over medium-high heat 5 minutes. Add corn kernels, chives, and taco seasoning mix; sauté 5 minutes or until tender. **Yield:** 4 to 6 servings.

Tee's Corn Pudding

prep time: 15 min. • cook: 40 min. • stand: 5 min.

This classic recipe has a rich, soufflelike texture without the hassle.

12	to 13 ears fresh corn, husks removed	1½	teaspoons salt
¼	cup sugar	6	large eggs
3	tablespoons all-purpose flour	2	cups whipping cream
2	teaspoons baking powder	½	cup butter, melted

1. Preheat oven to 350°. Cut kernels from cobs into a large bowl (about 6 cups). Scrape milk and remaining pulp from cobs; discard cobs.
2. Combine sugar and next 3 ingredients. Whisk together eggs, whipping cream, and butter in a large bowl. Gradually add sugar mixture to egg mixture, whisking until smooth; stir in corn. Pour mixture into a lightly greased 13- x 9-inch baking dish.
3. Bake at 350° for 40 to 45 minutes or until set. Let stand 5 minutes. **Yield:** 8 servings.

Test Kitchen Tip
To prepare corn, cut off tips of corn kernels, using a paring knife. It's best to use corn when it's at its ripest.

Corn Pudding

prep: 18 min. • bake: 42 min. • stand: 5 min.

Creamed corn baked in custard is a traditional Southern dish worth preserving.

9	ears fresh corn		2	tablespoons sugar
4	large eggs, beaten		2	tablespoons all-purpose flour
½	cup half-and-half		1	tablespoon butter, melted
1½	teaspoons baking powder		⅛	teaspoon freshly ground pepper
⅓	cup butter			

1. Remove and discard husks and silks from corn. Cut off tips of corn kernels into a bowl, and scrape milk and remaining pulp from cob with a paring knife to measure 3 to 4 cups total. Set corn aside.

2. Combine eggs, half-and-half, and baking powder, stirring well with a wire whisk.

3. Preheat oven to 350°. Melt ⅓ cup butter in a large saucepan over low heat; add sugar and flour, stirring until smooth. Remove from heat; gradually add egg mixture, whisking constantly until smooth. Stir in reserved corn.

4. Pour corn mixture into a greased 1- or 1½-quart baking dish.

5. Bake, uncovered, at 350° for 40 to 45 minutes or until pudding is set. Drizzle pudding with 1 tablespoon butter; sprinkle with pepper.

6. Broil 5½ inches from heat 2 minutes or until golden. Let stand 5 minutes before serving.

Yield: 6 to 8 servings.

Cucumber Sandwiches

prep: 10 min.

Cold cucumber sandwiches are one of the ultimate feel-good foods that strike a chord with ladies of all ages.

1 large cucumber, peeled, seeded, and grated
1 (8-ounce) package cream cheese, softened
1 tablespoon mayonnaise
1 small shallot, minced
¼ teaspoon seasoned salt
1 (16-ounce) loaf sandwich bread
Garnish: cucumber slices

1. Drain cucumber well, pressing between layers of paper towels.
2. Stir together cucumber and next 4 ingredients. Spread mixture over half of bread slices. Top with remaining bread slices.
3. Trim crusts from sandwiches, and cut in half diagonally. Garnish, if desired. Store sandwiches in an airtight container in refrigerator. **Yield:** 16 sandwiches.

make ahead • portable

Creamy Cucumber Soup

prep: 20 min. • chill: 4 hr.

English, or hothouse, cucumbers have thin skins, few seeds, and mild flavor. English cucumbers are sold wrapped in plastic, rather than coated in wax.

¾ cup chicken broth
3 green onions
2 tablespoons white vinegar
½ teaspoon salt
¼ teaspoon pepper
3 large English cucumbers (about 2½ pounds), peeled, seeded, and chopped
3 cups fat-free Greek yogurt*
Garnishes: toasted slivered almonds, freshly ground pepper, chopped red bell pepper

1. Process chicken broth, green onions, vinegar, salt, pepper, and half of chopped cucumbers in a food processor until smooth, stopping to scrape down sides.
2. Add yogurt, and pulse until blended. Pour into a large bowl; stir in remaining chopped cucumbers. Cover and chill 4 to 24 hours. Season with salt to taste just before serving. Garnish, if desired. **Yield:** about 2 quarts.

*Plain low-fat yogurt may be substituted. Decrease chicken broth to ½ cup.

Fried Cucumbers

Fried Cucumbers

prep: 10 min. • cook: 27 min. • stand: 20 min.

Kirby cucumbers are short (about 6 inches long) and very crisp, which makes them ideal for pickling and frying.

4 small Kirby cucumbers (about 1 pound), cut into ⅛- to ¼-inch-thick slices
1 teaspoon kosher salt, divided
¾ cup cornstarch
½ cup self-rising white cornmeal mix
¼ teaspoon ground black pepper
¼ teaspoon ground red pepper
¾ cup lemon-lime soft drink
1 large egg, lightly beaten
Vegetable oil
Ranch dressing or desired sauce

1. Arrange cucumber slices between layers of paper towels. Sprinkle with ½ teaspoon kosher salt, and let stand 20 minutes.

2. Combine cornstarch and next 3 ingredients. Stir in soft drink and egg. Dip cucumber slices into batter.

3. Pour oil to depth of ½ inch into a large cast-iron or heavy skillet; heat to 375°. Fry cucumbers, 6 to 8 at a time, about 1½ minutes on each side or until golden. Drain on paper towels. Sprinkle with remaining ½ teaspoon kosher salt, and serve immediately with dressing or sauce. **Yield:** about 5½ to 6 dozen.

Note: We tested with White Lily Self-Rising White Cornmeal Mix.

Cucumber Salad

prep: 15 min. • stand: 2 hr. • cook: 3 min. • chill: 2 hr.

3 large seedless cucumbers, thinly sliced
2 celery ribs, thinly sliced
1 small green bell pepper, thinly sliced
1 small red bell pepper, thinly sliced
1 large red onion, thinly sliced
1 ½ tablespoons salt
1 cup sugar
1 cup white vinegar
1 teaspoon celery seed
½ teaspoon mustard seed

1. Combine first 6 ingredients in a large glass bowl; let stand at room temperature, stirring occasionally, 1 hour. Drain.

2. Bring sugar and next 3 ingredients to a boil in a medium saucepan over medium-high heat. Boil, stirring constantly, 1 minute or until sugar is dissolved. Let stand 1 hour. Pour over vegetables. Cover and chill 2 hours. **Yield:** 12 servings.

make ahead

Grits and Greens

prep: 15 min. • cook: 1 hr.

Two classic Southern foods come together in this old-fashioned yet trendy recipe. Stir them together, or spoon them side by side on each plate. And don't forget the ham garnish; sauté it briefly for the best flavor.

1 cup whipping cream
4 cups chicken broth, divided
1 cup uncooked stone-ground grits
¼ to ½ cup milk or chicken broth (optional)
1 pound fresh collard greens
¼ cup butter

1 to 1½ cups (4 to 6 ounces) freshly grated Parmesan cheese
¼ to ½ teaspoon freshly ground pepper
Garnish: cubed cooked ham or chopped cooked bacon

1. Combine whipping cream and 3 cups chicken broth in a large saucepan. Bring to a boil, and gradually stir in grits.

2. Cook over medium heat until mixture returns to a boil; cover, reduce heat, and simmer 25 to 30 minutes, stirring often. Gradually add milk or more chicken broth, if necessary, for desired consistency.

3. Remove and discard stems and any discolored spots from greens. Wash greens thoroughly; drain and cut into ½-inch strips.

4. Combine greens and remaining 1 cup chicken broth in a large skillet; bring to a boil. Cover, reduce heat, and simmer 10 to 20 minutes or until greens are tender.

5. Add butter, cheese, and pepper to grits, stirring until butter and cheese are melted. Stir in greens, if desired; cook just until thoroughly heated. Or serve grits and greens side by side on each plate. Garnish, if desired. **Yield:** 6 to 8 servings.

Creamed Collards

prep: 20 min. • cook: 40 min.

4½	pounds fresh collard greens*	½	cup apple cider vinegar
1	pound bacon, chopped	1	teaspoon salt
¼	cup butter	½	teaspoon pepper
2	large onions, diced		Béchamel Sauce
3	cups chicken broth		

1. Rinse collard greens. Trim and discard thick stems from bottom of collard green leaves (about 2 inches); coarsely chop collards.

2. Cook bacon, in batches, in an 8-quart stock pot over medium heat 10 to 12 minutes or until crisp. Remove bacon with a slotted spoon, and drain on paper towels, reserving drippings in stock pot. Reserve ¼ cup bacon.

3. Add butter and onions to hot drippings in skillet. Sauté onions 8 minutes or until tender. Add collards, in batches, and cook, stirring occasionally, 5 minutes or until wilted. Stir in chicken broth, next 3 ingredients, and remaining bacon.

4. Bring to a boil. Reduce heat to low, and cook, stirring occasionally, 15 minutes or to desired degree of tenderness. Drain collards, reserving 1 cup liquid.

5. Stir in Béchamel Sauce. Stir in reserved cooking liquid, ¼ cup at a time, to desired consistency. Transfer to a serving dish, and sprinkle with reserved ¼ cup bacon. **Yield:** 8 to 10 servings.

*2 (1-pound) packages fresh collard greens, washed, trimmed, and chopped, may be substituted.

Béchamel Sauce

prep: 10 min. • cook: 9 min.

Béchamel (bay-shah-MEHL) is the French term for white sauce.

⅓	cup butter	4	cups milk
2	medium shallots, minced	½	teaspoon salt
2	garlic cloves, pressed	½	teaspoon pepper
¾	cup all-purpose flour	¼	teaspoon ground nutmeg

1. Melt butter in a heavy saucepan over low heat; add shallots and garlic, and sauté 1 minute. Whisk in flour until smooth. Cook 1 minute, whisking constantly.

2. Increase heat to medium. Gradually whisk in milk; cook over medium heat, whisking constantly, 5 to 7 minutes or until mixture is thickened and bubbly. Stir in salt, pepper, and nutmeg. **Yield:** about 4½ cups.

Note: Mixture can be made ahead and stored in an airtight container in the refrigerator up to 2 days. Warm sauce over low heat before using.

make ahead

Crunchy Fried Okra

Southern-Style Collard Greens

prep: 15 min. • cook: 2 hr., 19 min.

12	hickory-smoked bacon slices, finely chopped	3	(1-pound) packages fresh collard greens, washed and trimmed
2	medium-size sweet onions, finely chopped	⅓	cup apple cider vinegar
¾	pound smoked ham, chopped	1	tablespoon sugar
6	garlic cloves, finely chopped	1	teaspoon salt
3	(32-ounce) containers chicken broth	¾	teaspoon pepper

1. Cook bacon in a 10-quart stockpot over medium heat 10 to 12 minutes or until almost crisp. Add onions, and sauté 8 minutes; add ham and garlic, and sauté 1 minute. Stir in broth and remaining ingredients. Cook 2 hours or to desired degree of tenderness. **Yield:** 10 to 12 servings.

Crunchy Fried Okra

prep: 20 min. • cook: 2 min. per batch

Whole okra, halved lengthwise, gives a fun twist to this fried favorite.

	Peanut oil	1½	cups all-purpose flour
1½	cups buttermilk	1	teaspoon salt
1	large egg	1	pound fresh okra, cut in half lengthwise
2	cups saltine cracker crumbs (2 sleeves)		Salt (optional)

1. Pour oil to a depth of 2 inches into a Dutch oven or cast-iron skillet; heat to 375°.
2. Stir together buttermilk and egg. Combine cracker crumbs, flour, and salt. Dip okra pieces in buttermilk mixture; dredge in cracker crumb mixture.
3. Fry okra, in 3 batches, 2 minutes or until golden, turning once. Drain on paper towels. Sprinkle lightly with salt, if desired. **Yield:** 4 to 6 servings.

Okra and Tomatoes

prep: 25 min. • cook: 20 min.

Juicy, summer-ripe tomatoes make this dish shine. You can use a large can of San Marzano tomatoes, chopped, as an out-of-season option.

4	bacon slices		1	teaspoon salt
1	large sweet onion, chopped		1	teaspoon pepper
3	large tomatoes, chopped		1	garlic clove, minced
1	pound fresh okra, chopped			Hot cooked rice

1. Cook bacon in a large skillet or Dutch oven over medium heat until crisp. Remove and crumble bacon; reserve 2 tablespoons drippings in skillet.
2. Sauté onion in hot drippings over medium-high heat 5 minutes or until tender. Stir in tomatoes and next 4 ingredients. Reduce heat, and cook, stirring often, 10 minutes or until okra is tender. Serve over rice, and sprinkle with bacon. **Yield:** 8 servings.

Grilled Okra and Tomatoes

prep: 10 min. • grill: 5 min.

1	pound fresh okra, trimmed		½	teaspoon salt
1	pint cherry tomatoes		½	teaspoon pepper
2	tablespoons olive oil		2	tablespoons chopped fresh basil

1. Preheat grill to 350° to 400° (medium-high) heat.
2. Combine first 5 ingredients in a large bowl.
3. Place mixture on cooking grate; grill, covered with grill lid. Grill tomatoes 3 minutes or just until they begin to pop. Turn okra, and grill, covered with grill lid, 2 to 3 more minutes or until tender.
4. Transfer okra and tomatoes to a serving dish, and sprinkle with basil. Serve immediately. **Yield:** 4 servings.

Okra and Tomatoes

Green Peas With Crispy Bacon

prep: 20 min. • cook: 17 min.

Mint and orange brighten the flavor of this simple side dish. Early in the season, while you can, use fresh peas. Boy, are they ever good!

4	bacon slices		½	teaspoon salt
2	shallots, sliced		2	(16-ounce) packages frozen sweet peas, thawed*
1	teaspoon orange zest			
1	cup fresh orange juice		2	to 3 tablespoons chopped fresh mint
1	teaspoon pepper		1	tablespoon butter

1. Cook bacon in a large skillet over medium heat until crisp. Remove and crumble bacon; reserve 2 teaspoons drippings in skillet.

2. Sauté shallots in hot drippings over medium-high heat 2 minutes or until tender. Stir in orange zest, orange juice, pepper, and salt. Cook, stirring occasionally, 5 minutes or until reduced by half. Add peas, and cook 5 minutes; stir in mint and butter.

3. Transfer peas to a serving dish, and sprinkle with crumbled bacon. **Yield:** 12 servings.

*6 cups shelled fresh sweet peas may be substituted. Cook peas in boiling water to cover 5 minutes; drain and proceed with recipe as directed.

" Peas lose **sweetness** as their natural sugars turn to starch during storage. Store them dry and unwashed in plastic bags in the refrigerator, and use as soon as possible. "

Two-Cheese Squash Casserole

prep: 25 min. • bake: 43 min.

For a flavorful, colorful twist, substitute sliced zucchini for half of the yellow squash.

4	pounds yellow squash, sliced		1	teaspoon freshly ground pepper
1	large sweet onion, finely chopped		2	large eggs, lightly beaten
1	cup (4 ounces) shredded Cheddar cheese		2½	cups soft, fresh breadcrumbs, divided
½	cup chopped fresh chives		1¼	cups (5 ounces) freshly shredded Parmesan cheese, divided
1	(8-ounce) container sour cream			
1	teaspoon garlic salt		2	tablespoons butter, melted

1. Preheat oven to 350°. Cook yellow squash and onion in boiling water to cover in a Dutch oven 8 minutes or just until tender; drain squash mixture well.

2. Combine squash mixture, Cheddar cheese, next 5 ingredients, 1 cup breadcrumbs, and ¾ cup Parmesan cheese. Spoon into a lightly greased 13- x 9-inch baking dish.

3. Stir together melted butter and remaining 1½ cups breadcrumbs and ½ cup Parmesan cheese. Sprinkle breadcrumb mixture over top of casserole.

4. Bake at 350° for 35 to 40 minutes or until set. **Yield:** 10 to 12 servings.

Squash casserole is the most **versatile** side dish. It pairs with everything from fried chicken in the summertime to turkey at Thanksgiving.

Summer Squash Casserole

prep: 25 min. • cook: 5 min. • bake: 30 min. • stand: 10 min.

There's just something about a classic vegetable casserole that's impossible to resist. Even picky eaters go back for second helpings.

1½	pounds yellow squash
1	pound zucchini
1	small sweet onion, chopped
2½	teaspoons salt, divided
1	cup grated carrots
1	(10¾-ounce) can cream of chicken soup

1	(8-ounce) container sour cream
1	(8-ounce) can water chestnuts, drained and chopped
1	(8-ounce) bag herb-seasoned stuffing*
½	cup butter, melted

1. Preheat oven to 350°. Cut squash and zucchini into ¼-inch-thick slices; place in a Dutch oven. Add chopped onion, 2 teaspoons salt, and water to cover. Bring to a boil over medium-high heat, and cook 5 minutes; drain well.

2. Stir together grated carrots, next 3 ingredients, and remaining ½ teaspoon salt in a large bowl; fold in squash mixture. Stir together stuffing and melted butter; spoon half of stuffing mixture into bottom of a lightly greased 13- x 9-inch baking dish. Spoon squash mixture over stuffing mixture, and top with remaining stuffing mixture.

3. Bake at 350° for 30 to 35 minutes or until bubbly and golden brown, shielding with aluminum foil after 20 to 25 minutes to prevent excessive browning, if necessary. Let stand 10 minutes before serving. **Yield:** 8 servings.

Crumb-Topped Spinach Casserole

prep: 13 min. • cook: 8 min. • bake: 30 min.

This quick, cheesy side, with its crunchy browned topping, can be ready to bake in just over the time it takes to preheat the oven. It's the one to introduce kids to spinach.

2	tablespoons butter	½	teaspoon salt
1	medium onion, chopped	¼	teaspoon pepper
2	garlic cloves, minced	1	cup milk
4	(10-ounce) packages frozen chopped spinach, thawed	1	(8-ounce) package shredded Cheddar cheese
1	(8-ounce) package cream cheese, softened	1	cup Italian-seasoned Japanese breadcrumbs (panko) or homemade breadcrumbs
2	tablespoons all-purpose flour		
2	large eggs	3	to 4 tablespoons butter, melted

1. Preheat oven to 350°. Melt 2 tablespoons butter in a large nonstick skillet over medium heat. Add onion and garlic, and sauté 8 minutes or until tender.

2. Meanwhile, drain spinach well, pressing between paper towels to remove excess moisture.

3. Stir together cream cheese and flour in a large bowl until smooth. Whisk in eggs, salt, and pepper. Gradually whisk in milk until blended. Add sautéed onion, spinach, and Cheddar cheese, stirring until blended. Spoon into a lightly greased 11- x 7-inch baking dish.

4. Combine breadcrumbs and 3 to 4 tablespoons butter in a small bowl; toss well. Sprinkle over casserole.

5. Bake, uncovered, at 350° for 30 to 35 minutes or until thoroughly heated and breadcrumbs are browned. **Yield:** 8 to 10 servings.

Note: To make individual spinach casseroles, spoon spinach mixture into 8 (8-ounce) lightly greased ramekins; top each with buttered breadcrumbs. Bake, uncovered, at 375° for 25 to 30 minutes or until browned. (We found that a slightly higher temperature produced better results for individual casseroles.)

Feta-Stuffed Tomatoes

prep: 15 min. • bake: 15 min.

4   large tomatoes
4   ounces crumbled feta cheese
¼   cup fine, dry breadcrumbs
2   tablespoons chopped green onions
2   tablespoons chopped fresh flat-leaf parsley

2   tablespoons olive oil
¼   teaspoon salt
¼   teaspoon pepper
Garnish: fresh flat-leaf parsley

1. Preheat oven to 350°. Cut tomatoes in half horizontally. Scoop out pulp from each tomato half, leaving shells intact; discard seeds, and coarsely chop pulp.
2. Stir together pulp, feta cheese, and next 6 ingredients in a bowl. Spoon mixture into tomato shells, and place in a 13- x 9-inch baking dish.
3. Bake at 350° for 15 minutes. Garnish, if desired. **Yield:** 8 servings.

Fried Green Tomatoes

prep: 15 min. • cook: 6 min. per batch

Dipped first in buttermilk and then in a flour-and-cornmeal coating before frying, these tomatoes come out hot, crisp, and juicy.

4	large green tomatoes		1	cup all-purpose flour
1½	cups buttermilk		1	cup self-rising cornmeal mix
1	tablespoon salt		3	cups vegetable oil
1	teaspoon pepper			Salt to taste

1. Cut tomatoes into ¼- to ⅓-inch-thick slices; place in a shallow dish. Pour buttermilk over tomatoes. Sprinkle with salt and pepper.

2. Combine flour and cornmeal in a shallow dish or pie plate. Dredge tomato slices in flour mixture.

3. Fry tomatoes, in batches, in hot oil in a large cast-iron skillet over medium heat 3 minutes on each side or until golden. Drain tomatoes on paper towels. Sprinkle with salt to taste. **Yield:** 6 to 8 servings.

Arkansas Tomato Sandwiches

prep: 10 min.

1 cup mayonnaise	Summer Griddle Cakes
1 cup loosely packed fresh cilantro leaves	Tomato slices
1 teaspoon lime zest	Salt and freshly ground pepper to taste
1 tablespoon fresh lime juice	Salad greens
1 garlic clove	Red onion, thinly sliced

1. Process mayonnaise, cilantro leaves, lime zest, lime juice, and garlic in a blender until smooth. Spread mayonnaise mixture over warm Summer Griddle Cakes. Sprinkle tomato slices with salt and freshly ground pepper to taste, and sandwich tomato slices with salad greens and thinly sliced red onion between griddle cakes. **Yield:** about 8 sandwiches.

Summer Griddle Cakes

prep: 10 min. • cook: 25 min.

4 bacon slices	1 tablespoon sugar
1 cup finely chopped okra	1⅔ cups buttermilk
1½ cups self-rising white cornmeal mix	3 tablespoons butter, melted
½ cup all-purpose flour	2 large eggs, lightly beaten

1. Cook bacon in a large skillet over medium-high heat 8 to 10 minutes or until crisp; **remove** bacon, and drain on paper towels, reserving drippings in skillet. Finely chop bacon.
2. Sauté okra in hot drippings 3 minutes or until crisp-tender.
3. Whisk together cornmeal mix and next 5 ingredients just until moistened; stir in okra and bacon.
4. Pour about ¼ cup batter for each griddle cake onto a hot, lightly greased griddle or large nonstick skillet. Cook cakes 2 to 3 minutes or until tops are covered with bubbles and edges look dry and cooked; turn and cook other side 1 to 2 minutes or until done. **Yield:** 17 (3½-inch) cakes.

Tomato and Watermelon Salad

prep: 20 min. • stand: 15 min. • chill: 2 hr.

Combine sweet, juicy watermelon chunks with fresh tomato, onion, and a red wine vinaigrette for a salad that's the essence of summer.

5 cups (¾-inch) seeded watermelon cubes	1 small red onion, quartered and thinly sliced
1½ pounds ripe tomatoes, cut into ¾-inch cubes	½ cup red wine vinegar
3 teaspoons sugar	¼ cup extra virgin olive oil
½ teaspoon salt	Romaine lettuce leaves (optional)
	Cracked black pepper to taste

1. Combine watermelon and tomatoes in a large bowl; sprinkle with sugar and salt, tossing to coat. Let stand 15 minutes.

2. Stir in onion, vinegar, and oil. Cover and chill 2 hours. Serve chilled with lettuce leaves, if desired. Sprinkle with cracked black pepper to taste. **Yield:** 4 to 6 servings.

"This **quick and easy** side dish is perfect for summertime entertaining. Wow your guests with the unique flavor combination."

Strawberry-Pineapple Iceberg Wedges

Prep: 30 min.

Look for seeded melon halves in the produce department to save a little time.

1 (16-ounce) package fresh strawberries, hulled
½ medium pineapple, peeled and cored
½ medium honeydew melon
¼ small cantaloupe
2 tablespoons chopped fresh mint
1 head iceberg lettuce, cored and cut into 6 wedges
Kosher salt and freshly ground pepper to taste
Yogurt-Poppy Seed Dressing

1. Cut first 4 ingredients into ¼-inch pieces (about 2 cups each cubed strawberries, pineapple, and honeydew melon and 1 cup cubed cantaloupe). Toss with mint.
2. Arrange 1 lettuce wedge on each of 6 serving plates. Top evenly with fruit mixture. Sprinkle with salt and pepper to taste. Drizzle with Yogurt-Poppy Seed Dressing. **Yield:** 6 servings

Yogurt-Poppy Seed Dressing

Prep: 10 min.

Yogurt and honey replace the oil and sugar typically found in this classic for a healthful, here-and-now dressing. We prefer Greek yogurt for its thick, rich flavor, but plain yogurt can be substituted for a thinner dressing.

1 cup plain Greek or plain yogurt
2 tablespoons honey
2 tablespoons fresh lemon juice
1 teaspoon poppy seeds

1. Whisk together all ingredients in a small bowl. Store in an airtight container in refrigerator up to 5 days. **Yield:** 1 cup

Watermelon Rind Pickles

prep: 1 hr., 30 min. • cook: 1 hr., 30 min. • stand: 16 hr.

Don't toss that watermelon rind! Here's a novel condiment that's both spicy and sweet. These pickles belong on a picnic plate next to peas, fried chicken, and a biscuit.

1	large watermelon (about 7 pounds)	9	cups sugar
¾	cup salt	3	cups white vinegar (5% acidity)
2	quarts ice cubes	1	lemon, thinly sliced
1	tablespoon whole cloves	5	(3-inch) cinnamon sticks
1	tablespoon whole allspice		

1. Quarter watermelon; remove all pink flesh (if you haven't already eaten it). Peel green skin from watermelon rind. Cut enough rind into 1-inch cubes to yield 12 cups, and place cubed rind in a large container. Discard any remaining rind.

2. Stir together salt and 3 quarts water; pour over rind. Add ice; cover and let stand 8 hours. Rinse well, and drain.

3. Cook rind in water to cover in a Dutch oven over high heat 10 minutes or until tender. Drain and place rind in large container.

4. Place cloves and allspice on a 3-inch square of cheesecloth; tie with string.

5. Stir together sugar, vinegar, and 3 cups water in Dutch oven; add spice bag, and bring to a boil. Boil 5 minutes, and pour over rind in large container. Stir in lemon slices. Cover and let stand 8 hours.

6. Bring rind and syrup mixture to a boil in a Dutch oven; reduce heat, and simmer, stirring occasionally, 1 hour. Discard spice bag.

7. Pack rind mixture into hot jars, filling ½ inch from top. Add 1 cinnamon stick to each jar. Remove air bubbles; wipe jar rims. Cover at once with metal lids, and screw on bands.

8. Process in a boiling-water bath 10 minutes. **Yield:** 5 (12-ounce) jars.

Peppered Beef Soup,
page 243

soup for supper

Easy Chicken and Dumplings

prep: 10 min. • cook: 30 min.

Deli-roasted chicken, cream of chicken soup, and canned biscuits make a quick-and-tasty version of this favorite. One roasted chicken yields about 3 cups of meat.

1 (32-ounce) container low-sodium chicken broth
3 cups shredded cooked chicken (about 1½ pounds)
1 (10¾-ounce) can reduced-fat cream of chicken soup
¼ teaspoon poultry seasoning
1 (10.2-ounce) can refrigerated jumbo buttermilk biscuits
2 carrots, diced
3 celery ribs, diced

1. Bring first 4 ingredients to a boil in a Dutch oven over medium-high heat. Cover, reduce heat to low, and simmer, stirring occasionally, 5 minutes. Increase heat to medium-high; return to a low boil.

2. Place biscuits on a lightly floured surface. Roll or pat each biscuit to ⅛-inch thickness; cut into ½-inch-wide strips.

3. Drop strips, 1 at a time, into boiling broth mixture. Add carrots and celery. Cover, reduce heat to low, and simmer 15 to 20 minutes, stirring occasionally to prevent dumplings from sticking. **Yield:** 4 to 6 servings.

"This **down-home** favorite dish is a popular comfort food for families all over the South."

Lemon Chicken Soup

prep: 30 min. • cook: 1 hr., 45 min.

6 skin-on, bone-in chicken breasts
2 large onions, chopped
5 celery ribs, chopped
2 garlic cloves, minced
1 teaspoon olive oil
1 (1-pound) package carrots, sliced
4 teaspoons lemon zest

2 bay leaves
2 teaspoons salt
½ cup loosely packed fresh flat-leaf parsley leaves

Toppings: cooked barley, cooked green beans, lemon slices

make ahead

1. Bring chicken and water to cover to a boil in a Dutch oven over medium-high heat; reduce heat to low, and simmer 1 hour.

2. Remove chicken, reserving liquid, and let cool 15 minutes. Shred chicken.

3. Pour reserved cooking liquid through a wire-mesh strainer into a bowl, discarding solids; wipe Dutch oven clean. Add water to cooking liquid to equal 10 cups.

4. Sauté onions, celery, and garlic in hot oil in Dutch oven over medium-high heat 5 to 6 minutes or until tender. Add shredded chicken, cooking liquid, carrots, and next 3 ingredients. Cover, reduce heat to medium, and cook 20 minutes or until carrots are tender. Add parsley. Serve with desired toppings. **Yield**: 5½ quarts.

You can freeze this **comfort in a bowl** ahead. Serve this soup with an assortment of crackers.

Chicken Noodle Soup

prep: 25 min. • cook: 1 hr., 15 min.

Chicken soup still reigns as the ultimate food for the soul. This recipe is chock-full of good stuff. Use fresh vegetables instead of frozen if you prefer.

one-dish meal • portable

6	skinned, bone-in chicken breasts
1	celery rib with leaves
1¼	teaspoons salt
¼	teaspoon pepper
1	(16-ounce) package frozen mixed vegetables
1	small onion, chopped
¼	cup chopped fresh parsley or 1 tablespoon dried parsley flakes
2	(3-ounce) packages chicken-flavored ramen soup mix

1. Bring 3 quarts water and first 4 ingredients to a boil in a large Dutch oven. Cover, reduce heat, and simmer 30 to 40 minutes or until chicken is tender. Remove chicken, reserving broth in Dutch oven. Skin, bone, and shred chicken.

2. Add mixed vegetables, onion, and parsley to reserved broth. Cover and cook over medium heat 20 minutes. Add ramen noodles with seasoning packet, and cook, stirring occasionally, 5 minutes. Stir in chicken, and cook 10 minutes. Season to taste with salt and pepper. **Yield:** about 3 quarts.

Beer-Cheese Soup

prep: 15 min. • cook: 16 min.

2½	cups milk
1	(12-ounce) bottle beer, divided
2	(5-ounce) jars process cheese spread
1	(10½-ounce) can condensed chicken broth, undiluted
½	teaspoon Worcestershire sauce
2	dashes of hot sauce
3	tablespoons cornstarch

1. Combine milk and ¾ cup beer in a Dutch oven. Cook over medium heat, stirring constantly, 2 to 3 minutes or until thoroughly heated.

2. Add cheese spread and next 3 ingredients. Cook over low heat, stirring constantly, until thoroughly heated.

3. Combine cornstarch and remaining beer; add to cheese mixture. Simmer, stirring constantly, 10 minutes or until thickened (do not boil). **Yield:** 6 cups.

Note: We tested with Kraft Sharp Old English Cheese. If you prefer a soup with more of a bite, we suggest using a dark beer, such as Michelob Honey Lager.

Chicken Noodle Soup

"Baked" Potato Soup

prep: 21 min. • cook: 4 hr.

make ahead • portable • slow cooker

6   large baking potatoes, peeled and cut into ½-inch cubes (about 3¾ pounds)
1   large onion, chopped (about 1½ cups)
3   (14-ounce) cans seasoned chicken broth with roasted garlic
¼   cup butter
2½ teaspoons salt
1¼ teaspoons freshly ground pepper
1   cup whipping cream or half-and-half
1   cup (4 ounces) sharp Cheddar cheese, shredded
3   tablespoons chopped fresh chives
Toppings: cooked and crumbled bacon, shredded Cheddar cheese, sour cream

1. Combine first 6 ingredients in a 5-quart slow cooker.

2. Cover and cook on HIGH 4 hours or on LOW 8 hours or until potatoes are tender.

3. Mash mixture until potatoes are coarsely chopped and soup is slightly thickened; stir in whipping cream, 1 cup cheese, and chives. Serve with desired toppings. **Yield:** 12 cups.

Caramelized Onion Soup With Swiss Cheese-and-Basil Croutons

prep: 20 min. • cook: 43 min. • broil: 3 min.

French onion soup gets a flavor update with basil-flavored crusty croutons.

6   medium onions, halved and thinly sliced
¼   cup olive oil
4   garlic cloves, pressed
3   tablespoons beef bouillon granules
1   teaspoon pepper
1   teaspoon chopped fresh thyme

2   tablespoons dry sherry (optional)
1   (8-ounce) French baguette
1   cup (4 ounces) finely shredded Swiss cheese
2   tablespoons chopped fresh basil
2   tablespoons mayonnaise

1. Cook sliced onions in hot oil in a Dutch oven over medium-high heat, stirring occasionally, 20 to 25 minutes or until onions are golden brown. Add garlic, and cook 1 minute. Stir in 8 cups water, bouillon granules, pepper, and thyme. Add sherry, if desired. Bring to a boil. Cover, reduce heat to low, and simmer, stirring occasionally, 20 minutes.
2. Ladle soup into oven-safe serving bowls, and place on a baking sheet.
3. Cut baguette diagonally into 8 slices. Stir together Swiss cheese, basil, and mayonnaise. Spread mixture on 1 side of bread slices. Top soup with bread slices, cheese side up.
4. Broil 5 inches from heat 2½ to 3 minutes or until lightly browned. Serve immediately.
Yield: 8 cups.

Cream of Potato and Onion Soup

prep: 20 min. • cook: 1 hr., 40 min.

2 tablespoons butter
1 tablespoon olive oil
4 large sweet onions, chopped (about 5 cups)
1 teaspoon sugar
3 tablespoons all-purpose flour
1 (32-ounce) container chicken broth
1 (32-ounce) package frozen Southern-style cubed hash browns

½ teaspoon dried thyme
1 bay leaf
1 teaspoon salt
½ teaspoon pepper
1 cup grated Gruyère or Swiss cheese
1 cup half-and-half
Garnishes: chopped fresh chives, freshly ground pepper

1. Melt butter with oil in a large Dutch oven over medium heat. Add onions and sugar. Cook, stirring often, 45 to 50 minutes or until onions are caramel-colored.
2. Sprinkle onions with flour, and stir to coat. Add chicken broth. Bring to a boil over medium heat, and cook 20 minutes. Add hash browns and 2 cups water. Reduce heat to low, add thyme and next 3 ingredients, and simmer 30 minutes.
3. Stir in cheese and half-and-half; cook, stirring constantly, over medium heat 5 minutes or until cheese is melted. Remove bay leaf before serving. Garnish, if desired. **Yield:** 12 cups.

This soup makes a **big batch** so if you have leftovers you can enjoy it for lunch the next day.

Southern Tortellini Minestrone

prep: 20 min. • cook: 42 min.

1   medium onion, chopped
1   tablespoon olive oil
3   garlic cloves, chopped
2   (32-ounce) containers chicken broth
¾   cup dry white wine
2   (14.5-ounce) cans Italian-style diced tomatoes
1   (16-ounce) package frozen green beans
1   (16-ounce) package frozen chopped collard greens, thawed
3   tablespoons chopped fresh parsley
1   tablespoon chopped fresh rosemary
½   teaspoon dried crushed red pepper
1   (16-ounce) package frozen cheese-filled tortellini
Garnish: black pepper

1. Sauté onion in hot oil in a large Dutch oven over medium heat 8 minutes or until onion is tender. Add garlic, and cook 1 minute. Stir in chicken broth, white wine, and tomatoes; bring to a boil over medium-high heat. Add green beans, collard greens, and next 3 ingredients. Reduce heat to medium, and simmer, stirring occasionally, 15 minutes. Add pasta, and cook 10 to 12 minutes or until pasta is done. Garnish, if desired. **Yield:** 8 to 10 servings.

Black Bean Soup

prep: 20 min. • soak: 8 hr. • cook: 4 hr., 45 min.

1   (16-ounce) package dried black beans
3   chicken bouillon cubes
½   small onion
¼   small green bell pepper
6   garlic cloves, minced
2   tablespoons olive oil
1   teaspoon dried oregano
1   teaspoon ground cumin
1½   teaspoons sugar
1   teaspoon salt
½   teaspoon pepper
Garnish: minced red onion

1. Wash beans, and remove any foreign particles and debris.
2. Soak beans in water to cover in a 6-quart stockpot 8 hours. Rinse and drain beans.
3. Bring beans, 3 quarts water, and bouillon to a boil. Cover, reduce heat to low, and simmer 3 hours. Do not drain.
4. Process ½ small onion and bell pepper in a blender or food processor until smooth, stopping to scrape down sides.
5. Sauté garlic in hot oil in a large skillet over medium-high heat 1 minute. Add onion mixture, and cook, stirring constantly, 4 minutes.
6. Stir onion-and-garlic mixture into beans. Add oregano and next 4 ingredients. Simmer, uncovered, 1½ to 2 hours or until beans are tender and soup is thick. Garnish, if desired.
Yield: 8 servings.

Southern Tortellini Minestrone

Butternut Squash Soup

prep: 25 min. • cook: 50 min.

6   bacon slices
1   large onion, chopped
2   carrots, chopped
2   celery ribs, chopped
1   Granny Smith apple, peeled and finely chopped
2   garlic cloves, chopped
4   (12-ounce) packages frozen butternut squash, thawed
1   (32-ounce) container low-sodium fat-free chicken broth
2   to 3 tablespoons fresh lime juice
1½ tablespoons honey
2   teaspoons salt
1   teaspoon ground black pepper
⅛   teaspoon ground allspice
⅛   teaspoon ground nutmeg
⅛   teaspoon ground red pepper
¼   cup whipping cream
Garnishes: sour cream, fresh thyme sprigs

1. Cook bacon slices in a Dutch oven until crisp. Remove bacon, and drain on paper towels, reserving 2 tablespoons drippings in Dutch oven. Coarsely crumble bacon, and set aside.

2. Sauté onion and carrots in hot bacon drippings in Dutch oven over medium-high heat 5 minutes or until onion is tender. Add celery and apple, and sauté 5 minutes. Add garlic; sauté 30 seconds. Add butternut squash and chicken broth. Bring to a boil; reduce heat, and simmer 20 minutes or until carrots are tender.

3. Process squash mixture, in batches, in a blender or food processor until smooth. Return to Dutch oven. Add lime juice and next 7 ingredients. Simmer 10 to 15 minutes or until thickened. Garnish, if desired. Top each serving with bacon. **Yield:** 8 servings.

"A **simple garnish** of sour cream and thyme sprigs enhances the soup without overpowering it."

Lyda's Cream of Carrot Soup

prep: 20 min. • cook: 46 min.

The starch in the carrots naturally thicken this colorful and tasty soup. A dollop of sour cream mixed with fresh chives and ground pepper make an excellent garnish.

2 tablespoons butter
1 (1-pound) package baby carrots, chopped
1 (1-pound) package parsnips, peeled and chopped
1 medium-size yellow onion, chopped
½ teaspoon salt

¼ teaspoon freshly ground pepper
2 (32-ounce) containers chicken broth
⅓ cup uncooked long-grain rice
⅓ cup half-and-half (optional)
Toppings: sour cream, chopped fresh chives, freshly ground pepper

1. Melt butter in a large Dutch oven over medium heat; add carrots and next 4 ingredients; sauté 8 minutes or until onion is tender. Stir in chicken broth. Bring to a boil over medium-high heat. Reduce heat to medium, and simmer, stirring often, 20 minutes. Stir in rice, and cook, stirring often, 18 minutes or until rice is tender.

2. Remove from heat. Process mixture with a handheld blender until smooth. Stir in half-and-half, if desired. Serve with desired toppings. **Yield:** 8 cups.

Here's a delicious, low-fat way to get the kids to **eat their veggies**.

Basil Tomato Soup

prep: 30 min. • cook: 40 min.

2   medium onions, chopped
4   tablespoons olive oil, divided
3   (35-ounce) cans Italian-style whole peeled
    tomatoes with basil
1   (32-ounce) container chicken broth
1   cup loosely packed fresh basil leaves
3   garlic cloves

1   teaspoon lemon zest
1   tablespoon lemon juice
1   teaspoon salt
1   teaspoon sugar
½   teaspoon pepper
1   (16-ounce) package frozen breaded
    cut okra

1. Sauté onions in 2 tablespoons hot oil in a large Dutch oven over medium-high heat 9 to 10 minutes or until tender. Add tomatoes and chicken broth. Bring to a boil, reduce heat to medium-low, and simmer, stirring occasionally, 20 minutes. Process mixture with a handheld blender until smooth.
2. Process basil, next 4 ingredients, ¼ cup water, and remaining 2 tablespoons oil in a food processor until smooth, stopping to scrape down sides. Stir basil mixture, sugar, and pepper into soup. Cook 10 minutes or until thoroughly heated.
3. Meanwhile, cook okra according to package directions. Serve with soup. **Yield:** 15 cups.

Tomatoes and fresh basil **are the stars** of this classic soup that's topped with crunchy fried okra.

Pot Likker Soup

prep: 20 min. • cook: 4 hr., 3 min. • cool: 30 min. • chill: 8 hr.

2	(1-pound) smoked ham hocks	½	teaspoon salt
1	medium onion, chopped	¼	teaspoon dried crushed red pepper
1	medium carrot, diced	1	(14.5-ounce) can vegetable broth
1	tablespoon vegetable oil	½	(16-ounce) package fresh collard greens,
1	garlic clove, chopped		washed, trimmed, and chopped
½	cup dry white wine		Cornbread Croutons

1. Bring ham hocks and 8 cups water to a boil in a Dutch oven over medium-high heat. Boil 5 minutes; drain. Reserve hocks; wipe Dutch oven clean.
2. Sauté onion and carrot in hot oil in Dutch oven over medium heat 4 to 5 minutes or until tender; add garlic, and cook 1 minute. Add wine; cook, stirring occasionally, 2 minutes or until wine is reduced by half.
3. Add hocks, 8 cups water, salt, and crushed red pepper to onion mixture, and bring to a boil. Cover, reduce heat to low, and simmer 3 hours or until ham hocks are tender.
4. Remove hocks, and let cool 30 minutes. Remove meat from bones; discard bones. Transfer meat to an airtight container; cover and chill. Cover Dutch oven with lid, and chill soup 8 hours.
5. Skim and discard fat from soup in Dutch oven. Stir in meat and vegetable broth.
6. Bring mixture to a boil. Gradually stir in collards. Reduce heat, and simmer, stirring occasionally, 45 to 50 minutes or until collards are tender. Serve with Cornbread Croutons.
Yield: 6 to 8 servings.

Cornbread Croutons

prep: 10 min. • bake: 45 min. • cool: 1 hr.

2	tablespoons bacon drippings or	1	large egg
	vegetable oil	½	teaspoon salt, divided
1	cup self-rising white cornmeal mix	½	teaspoon pepper, divided
1	cup buttermilk		

1. Preheat oven to 450°. Coat bottom and sides of an 8-inch square pan with bacon drippings; heat in oven 5 minutes.
2. Whisk together cornmeal mix, buttermilk, egg, ¼ teaspoon salt, and ¼ teaspoon pepper; pour batter into hot pan. Bake at 450° for 15 to 17 minutes or until lightly browned. Turn out onto a wire rack; cool completely (about 30 minutes). Reduce oven temperature to 325°.
3. Cut cornbread into 1½-inch squares. Place on a baking sheet; sprinkle with remaining salt and pepper.
4. Bake at 325° for 30 to 35 minutes or until crisp and lightly browned. Remove to a wire rack; cool completely (about 30 minutes). Store in airtight container up to 1 day. **Yield:** 6 to 8 servings.

make ahead

Spiced Butternut-Pumpkin Soup

prep: 30 min. • cook: 30 min. • stand: 30 min.

Use an assortment of glasses to make appetizer-size servings of this tasty soup.

2 tablespoons butter	1 large Granny Smith apple, peeled and cubed
1 large sweet onion, diced	1 (32-ounce) container low-sodium chicken broth
1 large red bell pepper, chopped	
3 garlic cloves, minced	2 bay leaves
2 tablespoons finely grated fresh ginger	1½ teaspoons red curry paste**
1 medium butternut squash, peeled and cubed (about 1¾ pounds)*	½ teaspoon ground pepper
	¾ cup whipping cream
1 small pumpkin, peeled and cubed (about 1¾ pounds)*	1 tablespoon fresh lime juice
	Salt and pepper to taste
1 large sweet potato, peeled and cubed	

1. Melt butter in a large Dutch oven over medium-high heat; add onion and bell pepper, and sauté 8 minutes or until onion is golden. Stir in garlic and ginger, and cook 1 minute. Add squash, next 7 ingredients, and 4 cups water. Bring to a boil, reduce heat to medium-low, and simmer 20 minutes or until vegetables are tender. Remove from heat, and let stand 30 minutes, stirring occasionally. Remove and discard bay leaves.

2. Process soup, in batches, in a blender until smooth. Return to Dutch oven, and stir in cream. Bring to a simmer over medium heat; stir in lime juice, and season with salt and pepper to taste. **Yield:** 15 cups.

*3 pounds butternut squash may be substituted for 1¾ pounds butternut squash and 1¾ pounds pumpkin.

**1 teaspoon curry powder may be substituted.

Beef Vegetable Soup

prep: 15 min. • cook: 1 hr.

kids' favorite

1½ pounds beef stew meat
1 tablespoon olive oil
1 (32-ounce) bag frozen mixed vegetables (peas, carrots, green beans, and lima beans)
1 (15-ounce) can tomato sauce
1 (14.5-ounce) can Italian-style diced tomatoes
1 medium-size baking potato, peeled and diced

1 celery rib, chopped
1 medium onion, chopped
2 garlic cloves, minced
½ cup ketchup
1 extra-large chicken bouillon cube
½ teaspoon pepper

1. Cook meat in hot oil over medium-high heat in a large Dutch oven 6 to 8 minutes or until browned.

2. Stir in frozen mixed vegetables, next 9 ingredients, and ½ quart water, stirring to loosen particles from bottom of Dutch oven. Bring mixture to a boil over medium-high heat; cover, reduce heat to low, and simmer, stirring occasionally, 55 to 60 minutes or until potatoes are tender. **Yield:** 18 cups.

Test Kitchen Tip

When sautéing bite-size pieces of meat, stir frequently (but not constantly) to promote even browning and cooking. Portion-size cuts of meat should be turned only once so they have enough time to form a nice crust, which will also keep the meat from sticking to the pan.

You can serve this **hearty one-dish** meal with crusty French bread or grilled cheese sandwiches.

Peppered Beef Soup

prep: 20 min. • cook: 7 hr., 8 min.

Freeze leftovers in an airtight container up to 3 months. Add a bit of canned broth when reheating to reach desired consistency.

make ahead

1	(4-pound) sirloin tip beef roast
½	cup all-purpose flour
2	tablespoons canola oil
1	medium-size red onion, thinly sliced
6	garlic cloves, minced
2	large baking potatoes, peeled and diced
1	(16-ounce) package baby carrots
2	(12-ounce) bottles lager beer*

2	tablespoons balsamic vinegar
2	tablespoons Worcestershire sauce
2	tablespoons dried parsley flakes
1	tablespoon beef bouillon granules
1½	to 3 teaspoons freshly ground pepper
4	bay leaves
	Salt to taste

1. Rinse roast, and pat dry. Cut a 1-inch-deep cavity in the shape of an "X" on top of roast. (Do not cut all the way through roast.) Dredge roast in all-purpose flour; shake off excess.

2. Cook roast in hot oil in a Dutch oven over medium-high heat 1 to 2 minutes on each side or until lightly browned.

3. Place roast in a 6-quart slow cooker. Stuff cavity with sliced red onion and minced garlic; top roast with potatoes and baby carrots. Pour beer, balsamic vinegar, and Worcestershire sauce into slow cooker. Sprinkle with parsley, bouillon granules, and ground pepper. Add bay leaves to liquid in slow cooker.

4. Cover and cook on LOW 7 to 8 hours or until fork-tender. Remove and discard bay leaves. Shred roast using 2 forks. Season with salt to taste. **Yield:** 12 cups.

*3 cups low-sodium beef broth may be substituted.

30-Minute Chili

prep: 5 min. • cook: 25 min.

A homemade seasoning mix gives this quick chili great taste.

2	pounds lean ground beef
⅓	cup Chili Seasoning Mix
2	(14.5-ounce) cans diced tomatoes with green pepper, celery, and onion
2	(8-ounce) cans tomato sauce
1	(16-ounce) can black beans, undrained
1	(15.5-ounce) can small red beans, undrained
	Toppings: corn chips, shredded Cheddar cheese

1. Cook beef in a Dutch oven over medium-high heat, stirring often, 4 to 5 minutes or until beef crumbles and is no longer pink; drain well. Return beef to Dutch oven; sprinkle with seasoning mix. Cook 1 minute over medium-high heat.

2. Stir in diced tomatoes and next 3 ingredients; bring to a boil over medium-high heat, stirring occasionally. Cover, reduce heat to low, and simmer, stirring occasionally, 15 minutes. Serve with desired toppings. **Yield:** 8 servings.

Chili Seasoning Mix

prep: 5 min.

This versatile mix yields big dividends in time-saving suppers. Loaded with flavor, it pairs perfectly with beef, pork, poultry, or seafood.

¾	cup chili powder
2	tablespoons ground cumin
2	tablespoons dried oregano
2	tablespoons dried minced onion
2	tablespoons seasoned salt
2	tablespoons sugar
2	teaspoons dried minced garlic

1. Stir together all ingredients. Store seasoning mix in an airtight container up to 4 months at room temperature. Shake or stir well before using. **Yield:** about 1⅓ cups.

make ahead • portable • one-dish meal

Meatless Chili

prep: 5 min. • cook: 13 min.

This chili also works as a burrito filling. Just spoon some chili onto a warm flour tortilla, sprinkle with shredded lettuce and cheese, and roll up the tortilla.

Cooking spray

2 teaspoons jarred minced garlic

1 large onion, chopped

1 (16-ounce) can chili-hot beans, undrained

1 (14.5-ounce) can no-salt-added diced tomatoes, undrained

1 teaspoon chili powder

1 teaspoon ground cumin

12 ounces frozen vegetable and grain protein crumbles (about 3 cups)

Topping: oyster crackers

1. Coat a 4-quart saucepan with cooking spray. Place pan over medium-high heat. Add garlic and onion; sauté 3 minutes. Add beans and next 3 ingredients. Bring to a boil, stirring occasionally; reduce heat, and simmer 5 minutes. Add protein crumbles, and cook 3 minutes or until thoroughly heated. Top with oyster crackers, if desired. **Yield:** 4 servings.

This **chunky** dish is especially appropriate for the winter months. Sprinkle oyster crackers on top before serving.

Seafood Gumbo

prep: 1 hr., 5 min. • cook: 1 hr., 50 min.

This recipe serves a party crowd. It freezes well if you happen to have leftovers.

freezable • one-dish meal

2	lemons, sliced	1	pound cooked ham, cubed
1	(3-ounce) package crab boil	2	pounds fresh crabmeat, drained and flaked
1	teaspoon salt	3	pounds fresh okra, sliced
2	pounds unpeeled, medium-size raw shrimp	1	(28-ounce) can whole tomatoes, undrained and chopped
1	pound bacon	½	cup Worcestershire sauce
1	cup all-purpose flour	2	teaspoons salt
2	onions, finely chopped	1	teaspoon pepper
2	green bell peppers, finely chopped		Hot cooked rice
4	garlic cloves, minced		

1. Bring 1 gallon water, lemons, crab boil, and 1 teaspoon salt to a boil in a large Dutch oven. Add shrimp, and cook 3 to 5 minutes or until shrimp turn pink. Discard lemons and crab boil. Remove shrimp, reserving water. Peel shrimp. Chill.

2. Cook bacon in a large skillet until crisp; remove bacon, reserving drippings in skillet. Crumble bacon, and set aside.

3. Add flour to drippings in skillet; cook over medium heat, stirring constantly, until roux is caramel-colored (about 5 minutes). Stir in onions, bell peppers, and garlic; cook over low heat 10 minutes or until vegetables are tender.

4. Add roux, ham, and next 6 ingredients to reserved water in Dutch oven. Bring to a boil; reduce heat, and simmer 1 hour and 50 minutes. Stir in chilled shrimp, and cook 5 to 10 minutes. Serve gumbo over rice. Sprinkle with bacon. **Yield:** 7½ quarts.

Beef Daube

prep: 25 min. • cook: 3 hr., 28 min. • chill: 8 hr. • stand: 20 min.

Daube, a French country stew, is a homey dish made from simple ingredients. The secret to its rich flavor is to cook and cool it over a two-day period—a real bonus if you're looking for make-ahead menu options.

¼ cup olive oil or vegetable oil
1   (4-pound) boneless rump roast or chuck roast, well trimmed and cut into 1½- to 2-inch pieces
1½ teaspoons salt
1½ teaspoons freshly ground pepper
4   small yellow onions, cut into wedges
4   large carrots, cut into 2-inch pieces
1   garlic bulb, separated into cloves, each peeled and halved lengthwise
1   (14½-ounce) can Italian stewed tomatoes
1   (750-milliliter) bottle Cabernet Sauvignon; Côtes du Rhône; or other spicy, full-bodied red wine
Bouquet garni
Garnish: fresh thyme leaves

1. Heat oil in a Dutch oven over medium heat until hot. Sprinkle beef with salt and pepper. Cook beef in several batches in hot oil until browned on all sides. Remove beef to a large plate, reserving drippings in Dutch oven.

2. Sauté onions, carrots, and garlic in reserved drippings over medium heat 6 to 8 minutes. Add tomatoes and wine. Return beef to pan; add bouquet garni. Bring to a boil; cover, reduce heat, and simmer 1½ hours. Remove from heat, and cool completely. Cover pan, and refrigerate overnight.

3. Remove Dutch oven from refrigerator. Skim fat from surface, if desired. Let stew stand 20 minutes. Bring to a boil over medium heat; cover, reduce heat, and simmer 1 hour. Uncover and simmer 30 more minutes or until beef is very tender and stew is thickened. Discard bouquet garni before serving. Garnish, if desired. **Yield:** 6 to 8 servings.

Note: A bouquet garni is a small bundle of fresh herbs, such as parsley, thyme, and bay leaves, tied together with kitchen twine. We tested with flat-leaf parsley, rosemary, thyme, and 2 bay leaves.

Easy Brunswick Stew

prep: 15 min. • cook: 50 min.

Make preparation a breeze by stopping at your local supermarket deli or favorite barbecue restaurant for shredded pork.

3	pounds shredded cooked pork	1	(14½-ounce) can cream-style corn
4	cups frozen cubed hash brown potatoes	2	cups frozen lima beans
3	(14½-ounce) cans diced tomatoes with garlic and onion	½	cup barbecue sauce
		1	tablespoon hot sauce
1	(14½-ounce) can whole kernel corn, drained	1½	teaspoons salt
		1	teaspoon pepper

1. Stir together shredded pork, 4 cups water, hash brown potatoes, and remaining ingredients in a 6-quart stockpot. Bring stew to a boil; cover, reduce heat, and simmer, stirring often, 45 minutes. **Yield:** 5 quarts.

make ahead • one-dish meal

'Developed in **19th-century** Virginia, this traditional Southern stew originally included squirrel meat.'

Harvest Lamb Stew

prep: 20 min. • cook: 4 hr., 40 min.

2½	pounds lean lamb stew meat (about 1-inch pieces)
1½	teaspoons salt
¼	teaspoon freshly ground pepper
¼	cup all-purpose flour
4	tablespoons olive oil
1	(6-ounce) can tomato paste
1	(14.5-ounce) can beef broth

1	cup chopped celery
1	cup chopped sweet onion
3	garlic cloves, crushed
1	small butternut squash (about 1 pound), peeled, seeded, and chopped

Hot cooked mashed potatoes (optional)

Garnish: fresh parsley sprigs

1. Rinse lamb stew meat, and pat dry. Sprinkle with salt and pepper; toss in flour, shaking off excess.

2. Cook half of lamb in 2 tablespoons hot oil in a Dutch oven over medium-high heat, stirring occasionally, 10 minutes or until browned. Repeat procedure with remaining lamb and oil. Stir in tomato paste; cook 1 minute. Add broth, and stir to loosen particles from bottom of Dutch oven. Transfer mixture to a 6-quart slow cooker.

3. Stir in celery, onion, and garlic. Top with butternut squash. (Do not stir to incorporate.) Cover and cook on LOW 4½ hours or until meat is tender. Serve over hot cooked mashed potatoes, if desired. Garnish, if desired. **Yield:** 8 servings.

Variation

Harvest Beef Stew: Substitute 2½ pounds beef stew meat for lamb. Proceed with recipe as directed.

Test Kitchen Tip

To peel and cut butternut squash, use a sharp knife to cut 1 inch from the top and bottom of the squash; discard. Using a serrated peeler, peel away the thick skin until you reach the deeper orange flesh of the squash. With a spoon or melon baller, scoop away the seeds and membranes; discard.

**Triple-Decker Strawberry Cake,
page 288**

sweet treats

Ultimate Chocolate Chip Cookies

prep: 30 min. • bake: 10 min. per batch

If you like soft and gooey cookies, bake them for the minimum time. If you prefer crispy ones, bake them longer.

¾ cup butter, softened
¾ cup granulated sugar
¾ cup firmly packed dark brown sugar
2 large eggs
1½ teaspoon vanilla extract

2¼ cups plus 2 tablespoons all-purpose flour
1 teaspoon baking soda
¾ teaspoon salt
1 (12-ounce) package semisweet chocolate morsels

1. Preheat oven to 350°. Beat first 3 ingredients at medium speed with an electric mixer until creamy. Add eggs and vanilla, beating until blended.

2. Combine flour, baking soda, and salt in a small bowl; gradually add to butter mixture, beating well. Stir in morsels. Drop by tablespoonfuls onto parchment paper-lined baking sheets.

3. Bake at 350° for 10 to 14 minutes or to desired degree of doneness. Let cool on baking sheets 1 minute. Remove to wire racks, and cool completely. Store in airtight containers. **Yield:** about 5 dozen.

Variations

- **Pecan-Chocolate Chip Cookies:** Preheat oven to 350°. Bake 1½ cups chopped pecans in a single layer in a shallow pan 8 to 10 minutes or until toasted and fragrant. Proceed with recipe as directed, stirring in toasted pecans with morsels.
- **Oatmeal-Raisin Chocolate Chip Cookies:** Reduce flour to 2 cups. Proceed with recipe as directed, stirring 1 cup uncooked quick-cooking oats into dry ingredients in Step 2 and 1 cup raisins with morsels.

Chunky Chocolate-White Chocolate-Espresso Cookies

prep: 14 min. • bake: 21 min. per batch • cool: 5 min.

If you're looking for an amazingly good drop cookie, these thick cookies with soft white chocolate and a hint of coffee really hit the spot.

¾ cup butter, softened

1½ cups sugar

2 large eggs

1 teaspoon vanilla extract

2 (3.5-ounce) dark chocolate bars with finely ground espresso beans, chopped and divided

2¼ cups all-purpose flour

¼ cup cocoa

½ teaspoon baking soda

¼ teaspoon salt

2 (4-ounce) white chocolate bars, chopped

1 cup coarsely chopped pecan halves, toasted

1. Preheat oven to 350°. Beat butter and sugar at medium speed with an electric mixer until blended. Add eggs and vanilla, beating just until blended. Microwave half of dark chocolate in a small microwave-safe bowl at HIGH 50 seconds to 1 minute or until melted, stirring after 30 seconds. Add melted chocolate to butter mixture, beating just until blended.

2. Combine flour and next 3 ingredients; gradually add to butter mixture, beating just until blended after each addition. Stir in remaining dark chocolate, white chocolate, and pecans.

3. Drop dough by ⅓ cupfuls 2 inches apart onto lightly greased baking sheets.

4. Bake at 350° for 21 minutes. Let cool on baking sheets 5 minutes. Remove to wire racks, and cool completely. **Yield:** 15 cookies.

Soft Coconut Macaroons

Soft Coconut Macaroons

prep: 10 min. • bake: 18 min. per batch

4	egg whites	½	teaspoon clear vanilla extract
2⅔	cups sweetened flaked coconut	¼	teaspoon salt
⅔	cup sugar	¼	to ½ teaspoon almond extract
¼	cup all-purpose flour or matzo meal		

1. Preheat oven to 325°. Stir together all ingredients in a large bowl, blending well. Drop dough by teaspoonfuls onto lightly greased baking sheets.
2. Bake at 325° for 18 to 20 minutes or until golden. Remove to wire racks to cool completely.
Yield: about 3 dozen.

Test Kitchen Tip
Using clear vanilla extract will keep the macaroons pearly white, but if you don't have it, regular vanilla extract will work fine.

Tea Cakes

prep: 20 min. • chill: 1 hr. • bake: 10 min. per batch • cool: 5 min.

This Southern favorite just says summertime. For the best results, chill the tea cake dough thoroughly before you roll and cut it.

1	cup butter, softened	3½	cups all-purpose flour
2	cups sugar	1	teaspoon baking soda
3	large eggs	½	teaspoon salt
1	teaspoon vanilla extract		Parchment paper

1. Beat butter at medium speed with an electric mixer until creamy; gradually add sugar, beating well. Add eggs, 1 at a time, beating until blended after each addition. Add vanilla, beating until blended.
2. Combine flour, soda, and salt; gradually add flour mixture to butter mixture, beating at low speed until blended after each addition.
3. Divide dough in half; wrap each portion in plastic wrap, and chill 1 hour.
4. Preheat oven to 350°. Roll half of dough to ¼-inch thickness on a floured surface. Cut out cookies with a 2½-inch round cutter, and place 1 inch apart on parchment paper-lined baking sheets.
5. Bake at 350° for 10 to 12 minutes or until edges begin to brown; let cool on baking sheets 5 minutes. Remove to wire racks to cool. Repeat procedure with remaining dough. **Yield:** 3 dozen.

Sand Dollar Cookies

prep: 25 min. • chill: 2 hr. • bake: 14 min. per batch

Package a few sand dollar cookies for an extra treat to give to dinner guests when they leave. In Louisiana that's called a "lagniappe," meaning a little something extra.

1	cup butter, softened	½	teaspoon baking powder
2	cups sifted powdered sugar		Parchment paper
2	large eggs	¼	cup granulated sugar
1	large egg, separated	1	teaspoon ground cinnamon
3⅓	cups all-purpose flour		Sliced almonds

1. Beat butter at medium speed with an electric mixer until creamy; gradually add 2 cups sifted powdered sugar, beating until well blended. Add 2 eggs and 1 egg yolk, beating until blended.
2. Combine flour and baking powder. Add to butter mixture, beating at low speed until blended. Shape dough into a ball, and wrap in plastic wrap. Chill 2 hours.
3. Preheat oven to 350°. Roll dough to ⅛-inch thickness on a lightly floured surface; cut with a 3-inch round cutter. Place on lightly greased, parchment paper-lined baking sheets; brush with lightly beaten egg white.
4. Stir together granulated sugar and ground cinnamon, and sprinkle over cookies. Gently press 5 almond slices in a spoke design around center of each cookie.
5. Bake at 350° for 4 minutes; remove pan from oven, and gently press almonds into cookies again. Bake 10 more minutes or until edges are lightly browned. Remove cookies to wire racks, and cool completely. **Yield:** 4 dozen.

Test Kitchen Tip
To get ahead, chill the dough up to 3 days in advance. Before rolling, let it stand at room temperature about 30 minutes to soften.

Browned Butter-Pecan Shortbread

prep: 30 min. • bake: 6 min., plus 8 min. per batch • chill: 5 hr.

Buttery shortbread cookies are so tender they melt in your mouth. Toasted pecans and butter cooked until browned add a warm, cozy flavor that calls for a cup of hot tea or coffee and a few minutes to savor every bite.

1½ cups butter, cut into pieces	3 cups all-purpose flour
¾ cup firmly packed brown sugar	1½ cups finely chopped toasted pecans
¾ cup powdered sugar	

1. Cook butter in a large skillet over medium heat, stirring constantly, 6 to 8 minutes or until butter begins to turn golden brown. Remove pan from heat immediately, and pour butter into a shallow dish. Do not cover. Chill 1 hour or until butter is cool and begins to solidify.

2. Beat butter at medium speed with an electric mixer until creamy. Gradually add sugars, beating until smooth. Gradually add flour to butter mixture, beating at low speed just until blended. Stir in pecans.

3. Shape dough into 4 (8-inch) logs. Wrap logs tightly in plastic wrap, and chill 4 hours or until firm.

4. Preheat oven to 350°. Cut logs into ¼-inch-thick rounds; place on lightly greased baking sheets. Bake at 350° for 8 to 10 minutes or until lightly browned. Remove to wire racks, and let cool completely. **Yield:** about 10½ dozen.

Note: Finely chopping the pecans makes the logs easier to cut in Step 4.

> The **browned butter** in these cookies really helps to bring out the flavor of the toasted pecans.

Butter-Mint Shortbread

prep: 10 min. • bake: 20 min. • cool: 10 min.

A dash of mint extract gives these cookies an extra splash of flavor.

1	cup butter, softened	½	teaspoon vanilla extract
¾	cup powdered sugar	2¼	cups all-purpose flour
½	teaspoon mint extract		Powdered sugar

1. Preheat oven to 325°. Beat butter and ¾ cup powdered sugar at medium speed with an electric mixer until creamy. Add extracts, beating until blended. Gradually add flour, beating at low speed until blended. Press dough into an ungreased 15- x 10-inch jelly-roll pan.
2. Bake at 325° for 20 minutes or until golden. Cool in pan on a wire rack for 10 minutes. Cut into squares; sprinkle with powdered sugar. Remove to wire racks to cool completely.
Yield: 3 dozen.

For **ease,** you can't beat this recipe. The dough is pressed onto a jelly-roll pan, baked, and then cut into squares.

Lemon-Coconut Bars

prep: 10 min. • bake: 50 min.

The recipe for Lemon Chess Pie Filling is a Southern Living *favorite and the inspiration for this top-rated treat.*

freezable

2	cups all-purpose flour		½	cup chopped slivered almonds, toasted
1	cup powdered sugar, divided			Lemon Chess Pie Filling
1	cup butter, softened		1	cup sweetened flaked coconut

1. Preheat oven to 350°. Combine flour and ½ cup powdered sugar. Cut butter into flour mixture with a pastry blender until crumbly; stir in almonds. Firmly press mixture into a lightly greased 13- x 9-inch pan.

2. Bake at 350° for 20 to 25 minutes or until light golden brown.

3. Stir together Lemon Chess Pie Filling and coconut; pour over baked crust.

4. Bake at 350° for 30 to 35 minutes or until set. Cool in pan on a wire rack. Sprinkle with remaining ½ cup powdered sugar, and cut into bars. **Yield:** 32 bars.

Lemon Chess Pie Filling

prep: 10 min.

2	cups sugar		¼	cup fresh lemon juice
4	large eggs		1	tablespoon all-purpose flour
¼	cup butter, melted		1	tablespoon cornmeal
¼	cup milk		¼	teaspoon salt
1	tablespoon lemon zest			

1. Whisk together all ingredients. Use filling immediately. **Yield:** about 3 cups.

Double-Chocolate Brownies

prep: 15 min. • bake: 40 min.

Two kinds of chocolate lure you to try these rich brownies. No frosting needed.

freezable

2 (1-ounce) squares unsweetened chocolate	1 cup all-purpose flour
2 (1-ounce) squares semisweet chocolate	½ teaspoon salt
1 cup butter, softened	2 teaspoons vanilla extract
2 cups sugar	¾ cup chopped toasted pecans
4 large eggs	¾ cup semisweet chocolate morsels

1. Preheat oven to 350°. Microwave chocolate in a small microwave-safe bowl at MEDIUM (50% power) for 30-second intervals until melted (about 1½ minutes total time). Stir chocolate until smooth.

2. Beat butter and sugar at medium speed with an electric mixer until light and fluffy. Add eggs, 1 at a time, beating just until blended after each addition. Add melted chocolate, beating just until blended. Add flour and salt, beating at low speed just until blended.

3. Stir in vanilla, ½ cup pecans, and ½ cup chocolate morsels. Spread batter into a greased and floured 13- x 9-inch pan. Sprinkle with remaining ¼ cup pecans and ¼ cup chocolate morsels.

4. Bake at 350° for 40 minutes or until set. Cool completely on a wire rack. Cut into squares.
Yield: 32 brownies.

Note: Freeze brownies in an airtight container up to 1 month.

Mississippi Mud

prep: 10 min. • bake: 26 min.

The origin of this luscious dessert can be found both as a pie and as a cake. Either way, it's Southern decadence at its best and is featured here as a gooey brownie hunk.

1½	cups all-purpose flour		4	large eggs, lightly beaten
2	cups sugar		1	tablespoon vanilla extract
½	cup unsweetened cocoa		1	cup chopped pecans
2	teaspoons baking powder		3	cups miniature marshmallows
½	teaspoon salt			Chocolate Frosting
1	cup butter, melted			

1. Preheat oven to 350°. Combine first 5 ingredients in a large mixing bowl. Add butter, eggs, and vanilla, stirring until smooth. Stir in pecans. Pour batter into a greased and floured 13- x 9-inch pan.

2. Bake at 350° for 25 to 30 minutes or until a wooden pick inserted in center comes out clean. Immediately sprinkle marshmallows over top; return to oven, and bake 1 to 2 minutes. Remove from oven. Carefully spread Chocolate Frosting over marshmallows. Cool completely, and cut into squares. **Yield:** 2 dozen.

Note: For a hint of mocha, stir 1 tablespoon instant coffee powder into brownie batter along with dry ingredients.

Chocolate Frosting

prep: 5 min.

½	cup butter, melted		1	teaspoon vanilla extract
⅓	cup unsweetened cocoa		1	(16-ounce) package powdered sugar, sifted
⅓	cup evaporated milk			

1. Beat all ingredients at medium speed with an electric mixer until dry ingredients are moistened. Beat at high speed until frosting reaches spreading consistency. **Yield:** 2½ cups.

Cappuccino-Frosted Brownies

prep: 20 min. • bake: 30 min. • cool: 1 hr.

4   (1-ounce) unsweetened chocolate baking
    squares
¾   cup butter
2   cups sugar
4   large eggs
1   cup all-purpose flour

1   teaspoon vanilla extract
1   cup semisweet chocolate morsels
Cappuccino Buttercream Frosting
Garnish: chocolate-covered espresso beans,
    chopped

1. Preheat oven to 350°. Microwave chocolate squares and butter in a large microwave-safe bowl at HIGH 2½ minutes or until melted and smooth, stirring at 30-second intervals. Stir in sugar. Add eggs, 1 at a time, beating with a spoon just until blended after each addition.
2. Stir in flour and vanilla until blended. Stir in chocolate morsels. Pour mixture into a lightly greased 13- x 9-inch pan.
3. Bake at 350° for 30 to 35 minutes or until a wooden pick inserted in center comes out clean. Let cool completely on a wire rack (about 1 hour).
4. Spread Cappuccino Buttercream Frosting on top of cooled brownies. Cut into squares. Garnish, if desired. **Yield:** 10 to 12 servings.

Cappuccino Buttercream Frosting

prep: 10 min. • cool: 15 min.

1   (0.82-ounce) envelope 100-calorie café
    mocha cappuccino mix
¼   cup hot milk

½   cup butter, softened
1   (16-ounce) package powdered sugar
1   tablespoon cold milk (optional)

1. Stir together cappuccino mix and hot milk in a small cup until mix is dissolved. Cover and chill until mixture cools completely (about 15 minutes).
2. Beat milk mixture and butter at medium speed with a heavy-duty electric stand mixer until well combined. Gradually add powdered sugar, beating until smooth and fluffy. Beat in 1 tablespoon cold milk, if necessary, for desired consistency. **Yield:** 1½ cups.

Million-Dollar Pound Cake

prep: 20 min. • bake: 1 hr., 40 min. • cool: 1 hr., 10 min.

1 pound butter, softened	1 teaspoon almond extract
3 cups sugar	1 teaspoon vanilla extract
6 large eggs	Garnishes: sweetened whipped cream,
4 cups all-purpose flour	blueberries, sliced peaches
¾ cup milk	

1. Preheat oven to 300°. Generously grease and lightly flour a 10-inch (14-cup) tube pan. Use shortening to grease the pan, covering bottom. Sprinkle a light coating of flour over the greased surface. Tap out any excess flour.

2. Beat butter at medium speed with an electric mixer until light yellow in color and creamy. Gradually add sugar, beating at medium speed until light and fluffy. Add eggs, 1 at a time, beating just until yellow disappears after each addition.

3. Add flour to butter mixture alternately with milk, beginning and ending with flour. Beat at low speed just until blended after each addition. (Batter should be smooth.) Stir in extracts. Pour batter into prepared pan.

4. Bake at 300° for 1 hour and 40 minutes or until a long wooden pick inserted in center comes out clean. Cool in pan on a wire rack 10 to 15 minutes. Remove from pan, and cool completely on wire rack (about 1 hour). Garnish each serving, if desired. **Yield:** 10 to 12 servings.

Test Kitchen Tip

Beating butter with a mixer will cause it to become a lighter yellow color; this is an important step, as the job of the mixer is to incorporate air into the butter so the cake will rise. It will take 1 to 7 minutes, depending on the power of your mixer.

Cream Cheese Pound Cake

prep: 15 min. • bake: 1 hr., 40 min. • cool: 1 hr., 10 min.

This delicately crumbed cake received the highest possible recipe rating from our Test Kitchens staff.

1½	cups butter, softened	6	large eggs
1	(8-ounce) package cream cheese, softened	3	cups all-purpose flour
			Dash of salt
3	cups sugar	1	tablespoon vanilla extract

1. Preheat oven to 300°. Beat butter and cream cheese at medium speed with an electric mixer until creamy; gradually add sugar, beating well. Add eggs, 1 at a time, beating until combined.
2. Combine flour and salt; gradually add to butter mixture, beating at low speed just until blended after each addition. Stir in vanilla. Pour batter into a greased and floured 10-inch Bundt pan.
3. Bake at 300° for 1 hour and 40 minutes or until a wooden pick inserted in center comes out clean. Let cool in pan on a wire rack 10 to 15 minutes. Remove from pan to wire rack, and cool completely (about 1 hour). **Yield:** 10 servings.

Ginger Pound Cake

prep: 23 min. • cook: 5 min. • bake: 1 hr., 25 min. • cool: 1 hr., 20 min.

¾	cup milk	6	large eggs
1	(2.7-ounce) jar crystallized ginger, finely minced	4	cups all-purpose flour
		1	teaspoon vanilla extract
2	cups butter, softened		Vanilla bean ice cream
3	cups sugar		Garnish: crystallized ginger

1. Preheat oven to 325°. Cook milk and ginger in a saucepan over medium heat 5 minutes or until thoroughly heated (do not boil). Remove from heat, and let stand 10 to 15 minutes.
2. Beat butter at medium speed with an electric mixer until creamy; gradually add sugar, beating 5 to 7 minutes. Add eggs, 1 at a time, beating just until yellow disappears after each addition.
3. Add flour to butter mixture alternately with milk mixture, beginning and ending with flour. Beat at low speed just until blended after each addition. Stir in vanilla. Pour batter into a greased and floured 10-inch (16-cup) tube pan.
4. Bake at 325° for 1 hour and 25 minutes or until a wooden pick inserted in center comes out clean. Let cool in pan on a wire rack 10 minutes. Remove from pan to wire rack, and cool completely (about 1 hour). Serve with ice cream. Garnish, if desired. **Yield:** 10 to 12 servings.

Banana Pound Cake

prep: 20 min. • bake: 1 hr., 20 min. • cool: 1 hr., 15 min.

This moist, full-flavored banana cake needs no ice cream or sauce to enhance its appeal. But if you insist, we recommend pralines-and-cream ice cream.

portable

1½	cups butter, softened	2	teaspoons vanilla extract
3	cups sugar	3	cups all-purpose flour
5	large eggs	1	teaspoon baking powder
3	ripe bananas, mashed	½	teaspoon salt
3	tablespoons milk	¾	cup chopped pecans

1. Preheat oven to 350°. Beat butter at medium speed with an electric mixer about 2 minutes or until creamy. Gradually add sugar, beating 5 to 7 minutes. Add eggs, 1 at a time, beating just until yellow disappears after each addition.

2. Combine mashed bananas, milk, and vanilla.

3. Combine flour, baking powder, and salt; add to batter alternately with banana mixture, beginning and ending with flour mixture. Beat at low speed just until blended after each addition. Pour into a greased and floured 10-inch tube pan. Sprinkle with pecans.

4. Bake at 350° for 1 hour and 20 minutes or until a long wooden pick inserted in center of cake comes out clean. Cool in pan on a wire rack 10 to 15 minutes; remove cake from pan, and let cool completely on wire rack (about 1 hour). **Yield:** 10 to 12 servings.

Ripe bananas, with brown speckles on the yellow peel, add the best flavor. We often toss extra bananas in the freezer to keep on hand, but don't use them in this recipe—after thawing, their syrupy texture keeps the batter from rising properly.

Mama Dip's Carrot Cake

prep: 30 min. • bake: 47 min. • cool: 1 hr., 10 min.

This recipe from Chapel Hill, North Carolina, restaurateur Mildred "Mama Dip" Council makes one of the best carrot cakes we've tasted. The cake layers can be prepared ahead and frozen up to 1 month.

freezable • make ahead

2 cups chopped walnuts	2 cups sugar
2½ cups self-rising flour	1 cup vegetable oil
1½ teaspoons ground cinnamon	4 large eggs
1 teaspoon baking soda	3 cups grated carrots
Parchment paper	5-Cup Cream Cheese Frosting (page 287)

1. Preheat oven to 350°. Arrange walnuts in a single layer in a shallow pan. Bake 12 minutes or until toasted and fragrant.

2. Sift together flour, cinnamon, and baking soda. Line bottoms of 3 lightly greased 9-inch round cake pans with parchment paper; lightly grease parchment paper.

3. Beat sugar and oil at medium speed with an electric mixer until smooth. Add eggs, 1 at a time, beating until blended after each addition. Gradually add flour mixture, beating at low speed just until blended after each addition. Fold in carrots and 1 cup toasted walnuts. Spoon batter into prepared pans.

4. Bake at 350° for 35 to 40 minutes or until a wooden pick inserted in center comes out clean. Cool in pans on wire racks 10 minutes; remove from pans to wire racks. Peel off parchment paper, and let cakes cool 1 hour or until completely cool.

5. Spread frosting between layers and on top and sides of cake; sprinkle remaining 1 cup toasted walnuts onto cake as desired. **Yield:** 12 servings.

Red Velvet Layer Cake

prep: 15 min. • bake: 18 min. • cool: 1 hr., 10 min.

Classic red velvet cake holds memories for many people. Nowadays, there are red velvet cupcakes, cookies, cheesecakes, and sheet cakes, too. But above all, the three-layer cake stands tall and reigns supreme.

1	cup butter, softened	¼	teaspoon baking soda
2½	cups sugar	1	(8-ounce) container sour cream
6	large eggs	2	teaspoons vanilla extract
3	cups all-purpose flour	2	(1-ounce) bottles red food coloring
3	tablespoons unsweetened cocoa		5-Cup Cream Cheese Frosting

1. Preheat oven to 350°. Beat butter at medium speed with an electric mixer until creamy. Gradually add sugar, beating until light and fluffy. Add eggs, 1 at a time, beating just until blended after each addition.

2. Stir together flour, cocoa, and baking soda. Add to butter mixture alternately with sour cream, beginning and ending with flour mixture. Beat at low speed just until blended after each addition. Stir in vanilla; stir in red food coloring. Spoon cake batter into 3 greased and floured 8-inch round cake pans.

3. Bake at 350° for 18 to 20 minutes or until a wooden pick inserted in center comes out clean. Cool in pans on wire racks 10 minutes. Remove from pans to wire racks, and let cool 1 hour or until completely cool.

4. Spread 5-Cup Cream Cheese Frosting between layers and on top and sides of cake. **Yield:** 12 servings.

5-Cup Cream Cheese Frosting

prep: 10 min.

2	(8-ounce) packages cream cheese, softened	2	(16-ounce) packages powdered sugar
½	cup butter, softened	2	teaspoons vanilla extract

1. Beat cream cheese and butter at medium speed with an electric mixer until creamy. Gradually add powdered sugar, beating until fluffy. Stir in vanilla. **Yield:** about 5 cups.

Triple-Decker Strawberry Cake

prep: 25 min. • bake: 23 min. • cool: 1 hr., 10 min.

This cake from Anne Byrn, aka The Cake Mix Doctor, is so good no one will know it's not made from scratch. We doubled the frosting called for in Anne's original recipe to add extra richness.

make ahead

1 (18.25-ounce) package white cake mix	½ cup milk
1 (3-ounce) package strawberry gelatin	½ cup vegetable oil
4 large eggs	⅓ cup all-purpose flour
½ cup sugar	Strawberry Buttercream Frosting
½ cup finely chopped fresh strawberries	Garnish: whole and halved strawberries

1. Preheat oven to 350°. Beat cake mix and next 7 ingredients at low speed with an electric mixer 1 minute. Scrape down sides, and beat at medium speed 2 more minutes, stopping to scrape down sides as needed. (Strawberries should be well blended.)
2. Pour batter into 3 greased and floured 9-inch round cake pans.
3. Bake at 350° for 23 minutes or until cakes spring back when pressed lightly with a finger. Let cool in pans on wire racks 10 minutes. Remove from pans, and cool completely (about 1 hour).
4. Spread Strawberry Buttercream Frosting between layers and on top and sides of cake. Garnish, if desired. Serve immediately, or chill up to 1 week. **Yield:** 12 servings.

Note: We tested with Betty Crocker SuperMoist Cake Mix, White. To make ahead, prepare recipe as directed. Chill, uncovered, 20 minutes or until frosting is set. Cover well with wax paper, and store in refrigerator up to 1 week. To freeze, wrap chilled frosted cake with aluminum foil, and freeze up to 6 months. Thaw in the refrigerator 24 hours.

Strawberry Buttercream Frosting

prep: 10 min.

1 cup butter, softened	1 cup finely chopped fresh strawberries
1 (32-ounce) package powdered sugar, sifted	

1. Beat butter at medium speed with an electric mixer until fluffy (about 20 seconds). Add sugar and strawberries, beating at low speed until creamy. (Add more sugar if frosting is too thin, or add strawberries if too thick.) **Yield:** 2½ cups.

New-Fashioned Blackberry Chocolate Spice Cake

prep: 35 min. • bake: 30 min. • chill: 1 hr. • cool: 10 min.

Chocolate and spices mingle with sweet blackberries under a robe of chocolate fudge icing drizzled with blackberry sauce. Even traditionalists will be pleased with this updated classic.

Unsweetened cocoa
1 (18.25-ounce) package devil's food cake mix
1 (3.4-ounce) package chocolate instant pudding mix
3 large eggs
1¼ cups milk
1 cup canola oil
1 tablespoon vanilla extract
1 teaspoon chocolate extract
½ teaspoon almond extract

2 teaspoons ground cinnamon
¼ teaspoon ground ginger
¼ teaspoon ground nutmeg
¼ teaspoon ground cloves
2 (3.5-ounce) bittersweet dark chocolate with orange and spices candy bars, chopped
1 (21-ounce) can blackberry pie filling
2 (16-ounce) cans chocolate fudge frosting
Garnish: fresh blackberries

1. Preheat oven to 350°. Grease 2 (9-inch) round cake pans, and dust with cocoa. Set aside.
2. Beat cake mix and next 11 ingredients at low speed with an electric mixer 1 minute; beat at medium speed 2 minutes. Fold in chopped chocolate. Pour batter into prepared pans.
3. Bake at 350° for 30 to 32 minutes or until a wooden pick inserted in center comes out clean. Let cool in pans on wire racks 10 minutes. Remove from pans to wire racks, and cool completely (about 1 hour). Wrap and chill cake layers 1 hour or up to 24 hours.
4. Using a serrated knife, slice cake layers in half horizontally to make 4 layers. Place 1 layer, cut side up, on cake plate. Spread one-third of blackberry filling over cake. Repeat procedure twice. Place final cake layer on top of cake, cut side down. Spread chocolate fudge frosting on top and sides of cake. Drizzle remaining filling over top of cake, letting it drip down sides of cake. Cover and chill in refrigerator until ready to serve. Just before serving, garnish, if desired. **Yield:** 12 servings.

Note: We tested with Betty Crocker for cake mix and Green and Black's Organic for bittersweet dark chocolate.

Test Kitchen Tip
As a general rule in cake baking, grease cake pans with shortening unless the recipe states otherwise.

Fig Cake

prep: 20 min. • bake: 43 min. • cool: 1 hr., 10 min.

1 cup chopped pecans	1 teaspoon salt
3 large eggs	1 teaspoon ground cinnamon
1 cup sugar	½ teaspoon ground cloves
1 cup vegetable oil	½ teaspoon ground nutmeg
½ cup buttermilk	½ cup fig preserves
1 teaspoon vanilla extract	½ cup applesauce
2 cups all-purpose flour	Honey-Cream Cheese Frosting
1 teaspoon baking soda	Garnishes: dried figs, fresh mint sprigs

1. Preheat oven to 350°. Arrange pecans in a single layer in a shallow pan. Bake 8 minutes or until toasted and fragrant.

2. Beat eggs, sugar, and oil at medium speed with an electric mixer until blended. Add buttermilk and vanilla; beat well.

3. Combine flour and next 5 ingredients; gradually add to buttermilk mixture, beating until blended. Fold in fig preserves, applesauce, and toasted pecans. (Batter will be thin.) Pour into 2 greased and floured 8-inch round cake pans.

4. Bake at 350° for 35 to 40 minutes or until a wooden pick inserted in center comes out clean. Let cool on wire racks 10 minutes. Remove from pans to wire racks, and cool completely (about 1 hour).

5. Spread Honey-Cream Cheese Frosting between layers and on top and sides of cake. Store cake in refrigerator. Garnish, if desired. **Yield:** 6 to 8 servings.

Note: We tested with Braswell's Fig Preserves. Coarsely chop figs in preserves, if necessary.

Honey-Cream Cheese Frosting

prep: 10 min.

1½ (8-ounce) packages cream cheese, softened	1½ tablespoons honey
⅓ cup butter, softened	2 cups sifted powdered sugar

1. Beat cream cheese, butter, and honey at medium speed with an electric mixer just until smooth. Gradually add powdered sugar, beating at low speed just until blended. **Yield:** 3½ cups.

White Chocolate-Raspberry Cheesecake

prep: 22 min. • bake: 58 min. • chill: 8 hr.

Raspberry preserves make a luscious layer within this cheesecake.

make ahead

2 cups graham cracker crumbs
3 tablespoons sugar
½ cup butter, melted
5 (8-ounce) packages cream cheese, softened
1 cup sugar

2 large eggs
1 tablespoon vanilla extract
12 ounces white chocolate, melted and cooled slightly
¾ cup raspberry preserves
Garnish: fresh raspberries

1. Preheat oven to 350°. Combine first 3 ingredients; press crumb mixture into bottom of a lightly greased 9-inch springform pan. Bake at 350° for 8 minutes; cool slightly.

2. Beat cream cheese at medium speed with an electric mixer until creamy; gradually add 1 cup sugar, beating well. Add eggs, 1 at a time, beating after each addition. Stir in vanilla. Add melted white chocolate, beating well.

3. Microwave raspberry preserves in a small microwave-safe bowl at HIGH 30 seconds to 1 minute or until melted; stir well.

4. Spoon half of cream cheese batter into prepared crust; spread a little more than half of melted preserves over batter, leaving a ¾-inch border. Spoon remaining cream cheese batter around edges of pan, spreading toward the center. Cover remaining raspberry preserves, and chill.

5. Bake at 350° for 50 minutes or until cheesecake is just set and slightly browned. Remove from oven; cool completely on a wire rack. Cover and chill at least 8 hours.

6. Run a knife around edge of pan, and release sides. Reheat remaining preserves briefly in microwave to melt. Pour preserves over top of cheesecake, leaving a 1-inch border. Remove sides of pan. Garnish each serving, if desired. Store in refrigerator. **Yield:** 12 servings.

Note: To remove seeds from raspberry preserves, press preserves through a fine sieve using the back of a spoon, if desired.

German Chocolate Cheesecake

prep: 30 min. • bake: 45 min. • chill: 8 hr. • cook: 7 min.

With a nod to the classic three-layer cake, this luscious cheesecake takeoff comes pretty close to perfection.

make ahead

1	cup chocolate wafer crumbs
2	tablespoons sugar
3	tablespoons butter, melted
3	(8-ounce) packages cream cheese, softened
¾	cup sugar
¼	cup unsweetened cocoa
2	teaspoons vanilla extract
3	large eggs
⅓	cup evaporated milk
⅓	cup sugar
¼	cup butter
1	large egg, lightly beaten
½	teaspoon vanilla extract
½	cup coarsely chopped pecans, toasted
½	cup organic coconut chips or flaked coconut

1. Preheat oven to 325°. Stir together first 3 ingredients; press into bottom of an ungreased 9-inch springform pan.

2. Bake at 325° for 10 minutes. Cool crust.

3. Increase oven temperature to 350°. Beat cream cheese and next 3 ingredients at medium speed with an electric mixer until blended. Add eggs, 1 at a time, beating just until blended after each addition. Pour into prepared crust.

4. Bake at 350° for 35 minutes. Remove from oven; run a knife around edge of pan. Cool completely in pan on a wire rack. Cover and chill 8 hours.

5. Stir together evaporated milk and next 4 ingredients in a saucepan. Cook over medium heat, stirring constantly, 7 minutes. Stir in pecans and coconut. Remove sides of pan; spread topping over cheesecake. **Yield:** 12 servings.

Warm Apple-Buttermilk Custard Pie

prep: 30 min. • bake: 1 hr., 10 min. • stand: 1 hr.

When fall rolls around and that first cool snap is in the air, celebrate with this comforting apple pie. Use your favorite pie-baking apple if you'd like.

½	(14.1-ounce) package refrigerated piecrusts	4	large eggs
¼	cup butter	2	tablespoons all-purpose flour
2	Granny Smith apples, peeled and sliced	1	teaspoon vanilla extract
¾	cup granulated sugar, divided	¾	cup buttermilk
¾	teaspoon ground cinnamon, divided	3	tablespoons butter, softened
¼	cup butter, softened	¼	cup firmly packed light brown sugar
1⅓	cups granulated sugar	½	cup all-purpose flour

1. Fit piecrust into a 9-inch pie plate according to package directions; fold edges under, and crimp. Prick bottom and sides of piecrust with a fork.

2. Melt ¼ cup butter in a large skillet over medium heat; add apples, ½ cup granulated sugar, and ½ teaspoon cinnamon. Cook, stirring occasionally, 3 to 5 minutes or until apples are tender; set aside.

3. Preheat oven to 300°. Beat ¼ cup butter and 1⅓ cups granulated sugar at medium speed with an electric mixer until creamy. Add eggs, 1 at a time, beating just until yellow disappears. Add 2 tablespoons flour and vanilla, beating until blended. Add buttermilk, beating until smooth.

4. Spoon apple mixture into piecrust; pour buttermilk mixture over apple mixture.

5. Bake at 300° for 30 minutes. Stir together 3 tablespoons butter, remaining ¼ cup granulated sugar, brown sugar, ½ cup flour, and remaining ¼ teaspoon cinnamon until crumbly. Sprinkle over pie. Bake 40 more minutes or until a knife inserted in center comes out clean. Let stand 1 hour before serving. **Yield:** 8 servings.

Classic Chess Pie

prep: 23 min. • bake: 56 min.

½ (14.1-ounce) package refrigerated
   piecrusts
2 cups sugar
2 tablespoons cornmeal
1 tablespoon all-purpose flour
¼ teaspoon salt

½ cup butter, melted
¼ cup milk
1 tablespoon white vinegar
½ teaspoon vanilla extract
4 large eggs, lightly beaten

1. Preheat oven to 425°. Fit piecrust into a 9-inch pie plate according to package directions; fold edges under, and crimp.

2. Line piecrust with aluminum foil, and fill with pie weights or dried beans.

3. Bake at 425° for 4 to 5 minutes. Remove weights and foil; bake 2 more minutes or until golden. Cool completely.

4. Reduce oven temperature to 350°. Stir together sugar and next 7 ingredients until blended. Add eggs, stirring well. Pour filling into prebaked crust.

5. Bake at 350° for 50 to 55 minutes, shielding edges with aluminum foil after 10 minutes to prevent excessive browning. Cool completely on a wire rack. **Yield:** 8 servings.

Banana Pudding Pie

prep: 20 min. • bake: 24 min. • cool: 1 hr., 30 min. • chill: 4 hr.

Pie just doesn't get any better than this tasty twist on banana pudding. Hang onto your egg yolks—you'll be using them in the Vanilla Cream Filling.

1	(12-ounce) box vanilla wafers		Vanilla Cream Filling
½	cup butter, melted	4	egg whites
2	large bananas, sliced	½	cup sugar

1. Preheat oven to 350°. Set aside 30 vanilla wafers; pulse remaining vanilla wafers in a food processor 8 to 10 times or until coarsely crushed. (Yield should be about 2½ cups.) Stir together crushed vanilla wafers and butter until blended. Firmly press on bottom, up sides, and onto lip of a 9-inch pie plate.

2. Bake at 350° for 10 to 12 minutes or until lightly browned. Remove to a wire rack, and let cool 30 minutes or until completely cool.

3. Arrange banana slices over bottom of crust. Prepare Vanilla Cream Filling, and spread half of hot filling over bananas; top with 20 vanilla wafers. Spread remaining hot filling over vanilla wafers. (Filling will be about ¼ inch higher than top edge of crust.)

4. Beat egg whites at high speed with an electric mixer until foamy. Add sugar, 1 tablespoon at a time, beating until stiff peaks form and sugar dissolves. Spread meringue over hot filling, sealing edges.

5. Bake at 350° for 10 to 12 minutes or until golden brown. Remove from oven, and let cool 1 hour on a wire rack or until completely cool. Coarsely crush remaining 10 vanilla wafers, and sprinkle over top of pie. Chill 4 hours. Store leftovers in refrigerator. **Yield:** 8 servings.

Vanilla Cream Filling

prep: 5 min. • cook: 8 min.

¾	cup sugar	4	egg yolks
⅓	cup all-purpose flour	2	cups milk
2	large eggs	2	teaspoons vanilla extract

1. Whisk together first 5 ingredients in a heavy saucepan. Cook over medium-low heat, whisking constantly, 8 to 10 minutes or until mixture reaches the thickness of chilled pudding. (Mixture will just begin to bubble and will be thick enough to hold soft peaks when whisk is lifted.) Remove from heat, and stir in vanilla. Use immediately. **Yield:** 2½ cups.

Coconut Cream Pie

prep: 20 min. • bake: 10 min. • cook: 11 min. • cool: 5 min. • chill: 4 hr.

In true diner style, this coconut pie has a thick, buttery filling and a mountain of whipped cream on top.

½	(14.1-ounce) package refrigerated piecrusts	3	tablespoons butter
½	cup sugar	1	cup sweetened flaked coconut
¼	cup cornstarch	2½	teaspoons vanilla extract, divided
2	cups half-and-half	2	cups whipping cream
4	egg yolks	⅓	cup sugar
			Garnish: toasted coconut

1. Preheat oven to 450°. Fit piecrust into a 9-inch pie plate according to package directions; fold edges under, and crimp. Prick bottom and sides of piecrust with a fork.

2. Bake at 450° for 10 to 12 minutes or until lightly browned. Cool crust on a wire rack.

3. Combine ½ cup sugar and cornstarch in a heavy saucepan. Whisk together half-and-half and egg yolks. Gradually whisk egg mixture into sugar mixture; bring to a simmer over medium heat, whisking constantly. Simmer, whisking constantly, 3 minutes; remove from heat. Stir in butter until it melts; stir in 1 cup coconut and 1 teaspoon vanilla.

4. Place saucepan in an ice-water bath for 5 minutes or until filling is slightly warm, gently stirring occasionally. Pour filling into prepared crust. Place plastic wrap directly on custard (to prevent a film from forming). Place pie in refrigerator for 4 hours or until thoroughly chilled.

5. Beat whipping cream at high speed with an electric mixer until foamy; gradually add ⅓ cup sugar and remaining 1½ teaspoons vanilla, beating until soft peaks form. Spread whipped cream over filling. Garnish, if desired. **Yield:** 8 servings.

Note: For dramatic effect, we garnished the pie with organic coconut chips. Find them at organic food stores. You could also use sweetened flaked coconut.

Lemon Meringue Pie

prep: 25 min. • bake: 30 min.

Get ready for some down-home comfort with this tangy-tart lemon pie featuring a flaky crust. To cut clean slices, dip your knife blade into cold water between cuts.

½	(14.1-ounce) package refrigerated piecrusts	6	egg whites
	Lemon Meringue Pie Filling	½	teaspoon vanilla extract
		6	tablespoons sugar

1. Preheat oven to 450°. Fit piecrust into a 9-inch pie plate according to package directions; fold edges under, and crimp. Prick bottom and sides of piecrust with a fork.

2. Bake at 450° for 10 to 12 minutes or until lightly browned. Cool crust on a wire rack. Reduce oven temperature to 325°.

3. Prepare Lemon Meringue Pie filling; remove from heat, and cover pan. (Proceed immediately to next step to ensure that meringue is spread over pie while filling is hot.)

4. Beat egg whites and vanilla at high speed with an electric mixer until foamy. Add sugar, 1 tablespoon at a time, and beat until stiff peaks form. Pour hot filling into prepared crust. Spread meringue over filling, sealing edges.

5. Bake at 325° for 20 minutes or until golden. Cool pie completely on a wire rack. Store pie in refrigerator. **Yield:** 6 to 8 servings.

Lemon Meringue Pie Filling

prep: 10 min. • cook: 10 min.

1	cup sugar	⅓	cup fresh lemon juice
¼	cup cornstarch	3	tablespoons butter
⅛	teaspoon salt	1	teaspoon lemon zest
4	large egg yolks	½	teaspoon vanilla extract
2	cups milk		

1. Whisk together first 3 ingredients in a medium-size heavy saucepan. Whisk in egg yolks, milk, and lemon juice. Bring to a boil over medium heat, whisking constantly. Cook, whisking constantly, 2 minutes; remove pan from heat. Stir in butter until it melts; stir in lemon zest and vanilla. **Yield:** enough for 1 (9-inch) pie.

Note: It's easier to remove the zest from lemons before juicing them.

Classic Strawberry Shortcake

prep: 20 min. • stand: 2 hr. • chill: 2 hr. • bake: 12 min.

This summertime favorite shows off juicy strawberries like no other dessert, though sliced peaches are equally nice as an option. If your berries are really sweet, decrease the sugar to suit your taste. Drop the dough easily by using a lightly greased ⅓-cup dry measure.

2	(16-ounce) containers fresh strawberries, sliced or quartered	4	teaspoons baking powder
¾	cup sugar, divided	¾	cup cold butter, cut up
¼	teaspoon almond extract (optional)	2	large eggs, lightly beaten
1	cup whipping cream	1	(8-ounce) container sour cream
2	tablespoons sugar	1	teaspoon vanilla extract
2¾	cups all-purpose flour		Garnish: fresh strawberries with leaves

1. Combine strawberries, ½ cup sugar, and, if desired, almond extract. Cover berry mixture, and let stand 2 hours.

2. Beat whipping cream at medium speed with an electric mixer until foamy; gradually add 2 tablespoons sugar, beating until soft peaks form. Cover and chill up to 2 hours.

3. Preheat oven to 450°. Combine flour, remaining ¼ cup sugar, and baking powder in a large bowl; cut butter into flour mixture with a pastry blender or 2 forks until crumbly.

4. Whisk together eggs, sour cream, and vanilla until blended; add to flour mixture, stirring just until dry ingredients are moistened. Drop dough by lightly greased ⅓ cupfuls onto a lightly greased baking sheet. (Coat cup with vegetable cooking spray after each drop.)

5. Bake at 450° for 12 to 15 minutes or until golden.

6. Split shortcakes in half horizontally. Spoon about ½ cup berry mixture onto each shortcake bottom; top each with a rounded tablespoon of chilled whipped cream and a shortcake top. Serve with remaining whipped cream. Garnish, if desired. **Yield:** 8 servings.

Blackberry Cobbler

prep: 12 min. • bake: 30 min.

1   cup sugar
¼   cup all-purpose flour
5   cups fresh blackberries or 2 (14-ounce)
    packages frozen blackberries, thawed and
    drained

1   tablespoon lemon juice
Crust
2   tablespoons butter, melted
1   teaspoon sugar

1. Preheat oven to 425°. Combine 1 cup sugar and flour; add berries, and toss well. (If using frozen berries, increase flour to ⅓ cup.) Sprinkle with lemon juice. Spoon into a greased 8- or 9-inch square baking dish.

2. Prepare Crust, and spoon 9 mounds over blackberries. Brush with butter, and sprinkle with 1 teaspoon sugar.

3. Bake, uncovered, at 425° for 30 minutes or until browned and bubbly. Serve warm with ice cream, if desired. **Yield:** 9 servings.

Crust

prep: 10 min.

1¾   cups all-purpose flour
3   tablespoons sugar
1½   teaspoons baking powder
¾   teaspoon salt

¼   cup shortening
½   cup whipping cream
½   cup buttermilk

1. Combine first 4 ingredients; cut in shortening with a pastry blender until mixture is crumbly. Stir in whipping cream and buttermilk just until blended. **Yield:** enough topping for 1 cobbler.

Bananas Foster Gratin

prep: 10 min. • cook: 4 min. • bake: 10 min.

Get all the flavor without the flame in this version of the famous dessert.

¼ cup firmly packed light brown sugar
1 tablespoon dark rum
¼ teaspoon ground cinnamon
2 teaspoons butter

4 medium-size ripe bananas
1 almond biscotti, crushed (about ⅓ cup)
Vanilla ice cream

1. Preheat oven to 450°. Stir together first 3 ingredients and 3 tablespoons water in a 10-inch skillet over medium heat; bring to a boil. Reduce heat to medium-low, and simmer, stirring constantly, 2 minutes. Remove from heat, and stir in butter.
2. Slice bananas diagonally. Add to brown sugar mixture in skillet, tossing to coat.
3. Spoon banana mixture into 4 lightly greased (1- to 1½-cup) gratin dishes or a shallow, lightly greased 1-quart baking dish.
4. Bake at 450° for 10 minutes or until bubbly. Remove from oven, and sprinkle with biscotti crumbs. Serve warm with vanilla ice cream. **Yield:** 4 servings.

Apple Brown Betty

prep: 15 min. • bake: 45 min.

4 cups soft white breadcrumbs
⅓ cup butter, melted
1 cup firmly packed brown sugar
1 tablespoon ground cinnamon

4 large apples, peeled and cut into ¼-inch-thick slices
1 cup apple cider

1. Preheat oven to 350°. Stir together breadcrumbs and butter.
2. Stir together brown sugar and cinnamon. Place half of the apple slices in a lightly greased 8-inch square baking dish; sprinkle apples with half of brown sugar mixture and half of breadcrumb mixture. Repeat procedure with remaining apples, brown sugar mixture, and breadcrumb mixture. Pour apple cider over top.
3. Bake at 350° for 45 to 55 minutes or until browned. **Yield:** 6 servings.

Apple Brown Betty

Sautéed Brown Sugar Pears

prep: 15 min. • cook: 7 min.

A simple skillet pear dish gets dressed up with crème fraîche and gingersnap crumbs. This recipe easily doubles to serve a crowd.

1   tablespoon lemon juice
3   Anjou pears, peeled and quartered
3   tablespoons butter
¼   cup firmly packed brown sugar

1   teaspoon vanilla extract
Crème fraîche or vanilla ice cream
Gingersnaps, crumbled

1. Sprinkle lemon juice over pears; toss. Melt 1 tablespoon butter in a large nonstick skillet over medium-high heat. Sauté pears 2 minutes or until browned. Add remaining 2 tablespoons butter and brown sugar to skillet. Reduce heat to medium-low; cook, stirring often, 3 to 4 minutes or until pears are tender. Remove from heat, and stir in vanilla extract. Serve warm pears and syrup with a dollop of crème fraîche or ice cream. Sprinkle with gingersnap crumbs. **Yield:** 4 servings.

Anjou pears are a **sweet fruit** with a firm texture, making them perfect for desserts like this one.

Bread Pudding With Rum Sauce

prep: 15 min. • bake: 50 min.

Day-old bread is best for soaking up the liquid in this comforting dessert. The easy Rum Sauce makes each serving luscious.

4	large eggs	6	cups torn, packed French bread
1½	cups sugar	1	large Granny Smith apple, peeled and chopped
3	(12-ounce) cans evaporated milk		
½	cup butter, melted	1½	cups coarsely chopped walnuts, toasted
1	tablespoon vanilla extract	1	cup golden raisins
2	teaspoons ground cinnamon		Rum Sauce

1. Preheat oven to 350°. Whisk eggs in a large bowl. Whisk in sugar and next 4 ingredients. Fold in bread and next 3 ingredients, stirring until bread is moistened. Pour into a greased 13- x 9-inch baking dish.

2. Bake, uncovered, at 350° for 50 minutes or until set. Cut into squares. Serve warm with Rum Sauce. **Yield:** 12 servings.

Rum Sauce

prep: 2 min. • cook: 3 min.

2	(14-ounce) cans sweetened condensed milk	2	tablespoons dark rum
		1	tablespoon vanilla extract

1. Pour condensed milk into a small saucepan; cook over medium heat until hot, stirring often. Remove from heat, and stir in rum and vanilla. Serve warm. **Yield:** 2½ cups.

Creamy Rice Pudding With Praline Sauce

prep: 15 min. • cook: 50 min.

If you're a fan of pure and simple old-fashioned desserts, this dish is for you. The praline sauce takes it to the next level.

2	cups milk	½	cup sugar
1	cup uncooked extra long-grain white rice	1½	teaspoons vanilla extract
½	teaspoon salt	20	caramels
2¾	cups half-and-half, divided	½	cup chopped toasted pecans
4	egg yolks, beaten		

1. Stir together first 3 ingredients and 2 cups half-and-half in a large saucepan. Cover and cook over medium-low heat, stirring often, 35 to 40 minutes or until rice is tender.

2. Whisk together egg yolks, ½ cup half-and-half, and sugar. Gradually stir about one-fourth of hot rice mixture into yolk mixture; stir yolk mixture into remaining hot mixture. Cook over medium-low heat, stirring constantly, until mixture reaches 160° and is thickened and bubbly (about 7 minutes). Remove from heat; stir in vanilla.

3. Stir together caramels and remaining ¼ cup half-and-half in a small saucepan over medium-low heat until smooth. Stir in pecans. Serve praline sauce over rice pudding. **Yield:** 6 to 8 servings.

Chocolate Pudding

prep: 15 min. • cook: 16 min.

Here's a really rich but simple homemade pudding. A small serving will satisfy.

make ahead

⅓ cup cornstarch

4 cups whipping cream

1 cup sugar

1 cup semisweet chocolate morsels

1 tablespoon vanilla extract

⅛ teaspoon salt

1. Combine cornstarch and ½ cup water, stirring until smooth. Bring whipping cream to a simmer in a 2-quart saucepan over medium heat. Stir in cornstarch mixture, sugar, and remaining ingredients, stirring constantly until chocolate melts. Cook pudding, stirring constantly, 8 minutes or until thick and creamy. Serve warm or chilled. **Yield:** 5 cups.

Ultimate Chocolate Pudding

prep: 10 min. • cook: 10 min. • cool: 10 min.

Definitive in flavor and silky in texture, this pudding deserves a place in the chocolate hall of fame.

1¼ cups sugar

½ cup Dutch process cocoa

¼ cup cornstarch

½ teaspoon salt

2½ cups milk

⅓ cup unsalted butter, cut up

2 teaspoons vanilla extract

Unsweetened whipped cream

Chocolate-filled vanilla wafer sandwich cookies

1. Whisk together first 4 ingredients in a medium saucepan. Gradually whisk in milk. Cook over medium heat, stirring constantly, until pudding boils and is thickened (about 8 to 10 minutes). Reduce heat to medium-low, and cook 2 more minutes. Remove from heat; add butter and vanilla, stirring gently until butter melts. Place heavy-duty plastic wrap directly on warm pudding (to keep a film from forming); cool 10 minutes.

2. Serve warm, or chill until ready to serve. Top with whipped cream. Serve with cookies. **Yield:** 3½ cups.

Note: For rich chocolate flavor, order double-Dutch dark cocoa online at www.kingarthurflour.com. We tested with Pepperidge Farm Milano cookies.

Chocolate Pudding

Pound Cake Banana Pudding

prep: 20 min. • cook: 13 min. • chill: 6 hr. • bake: 15 min.

This recipe was inspired by the pudding served at the famous Mrs. Wilkes' Dining Room in Savannah, Georgia—a family-style, comfort-food restaurant to write home about.

4 cups half-and-half	3 tablespoons butter
4 egg yolks	2 teaspoons vanilla extract
1½ cups sugar	1 (1-pound) pound cake, cubed
¼ cup cornstarch	4 large ripe bananas, sliced
¼ teaspoon salt	Meringue

1. Whisk together first 5 ingredients in a saucepan over medium-low heat; cook, whisking constantly, 13 to 15 minutes or until thickened. Remove from heat; add butter and vanilla, stirring until butter melts.
2. Layer half of pound cake cubes, half of bananas, and half of pudding mixture in a lightly greased 3-quart round baking dish. Repeat layers. Cover pudding, and chill 6 hours.
3. Preheat oven to 375°. Prepare Meringue, and spread over pudding.
4. Bake at 375° for 15 minutes or until golden brown. Spoon into glasses, if desired. **Yield:** 10 to 12 servings.

Note: We tested with Sara Lee Family Size All Butter Pound Cake.

Meringue

prep: 10 min.

¼ cup sugar	4 egg whites
⅛ teaspoon salt	¼ teaspoon vanilla extract

1. Combine sugar and salt.
2. Beat egg whites and vanilla at high speed with an electric mixer until foamy. Add sugar mixture, 1 tablespoon at a time, and beat 2 to 3 minutes or until stiff peaks form and sugar dissolves. **Yield:** about 3½ cups.

Boiled Custard

prep: 15 min. • cook: 25 min.

Boiled custard conjures up thoughts of Christmas in many families. It's a simple delicacy that needs no adornment.

4 cups milk
6 large egg yolks
¾ cup sugar
2 tablespoons cornstarch

Dash of salt
2 teaspoons vanilla extract

1. Pour milk into top of a double boiler, and bring water to a boil. Heat milk until tiny bubbles begin to appear around edges of pan. Remove from heat, and set aside.

2. Beat egg yolks with a wire whisk until frothy. Add sugar, cornstarch, and salt, beating until thickened. Gradually stir about 1 cup hot milk into yolk mixture; add to remaining milk, stirring constantly.

3. Cook custard mixture in double boiler over low heat, stirring occasionally, 25 minutes or until thickened and a candy thermometer registers 180°. (Do not boil.) Stir in vanilla. Serve warm or cold. **Yield:** 4 cups.

Old-Fashioned Vanilla Ice Cream

prep: 10 min. • cook: 30 min. • freeze: 30 min.

6	large eggs, lightly beaten	¼	teaspoon salt
2⅓	cups sugar	2½	tablespoons vanilla extract
4	cups milk	3	cups whipping cream
2	cups half-and-half		

1. Combine first 3 ingredients in a large saucepan; cook over low heat, stirring constantly, 25 to 30 minutes or until mixture thickens and coats a spoon; chill.

2. Stir in half-and-half and remaining ingredients; pour into freezer container of a 5- or 6-quart hand-turned or electric freezer. Freeze according to manufacturer's instructions.

3. Serve immediately, or spoon into an airtight container; freeze until firm. **Yield:** 3½ quarts.

Classic Cola Float

Classic Cola Float

prep: 2 min.

Add cherry syrup or flavored soda to this kid-friendly quencher. It's even better topped with a maraschino cherry with a stem.

Vanilla ice cream
1 (12-ounce) can cola soft drink

¼ teaspoon vanilla extract

1. Scoop ice cream into a tall glass, filling half full. Top with cola, and gently stir in vanilla. Serve immediately. **Yield:** 1 serving.

Root Beer Float

prep: 2 min.

Use premium root beer and a high-quality vanilla ice cream to make the best dessert drink.

Vanilla ice cream

1 (12-ounce) can root beer

1. Scoop ice cream into a tall glass, filling half full. Top with root beer, and gently stir. Serve immediately. **Yield:** 1 serving.

Porter Float

prep: 2 min.

Dark beer gives the ice-cream float a new dimension.

Vanilla ice cream
3 to 4 tablespoons creamy porter or stout beer

Fresh raspberries
Fresh mint sprig

1. Scoop ice cream into a tall glass, filling two-thirds full. Top with a few tablespoonfuls of beer. Top with raspberries and a mint sprig. **Yield:** 1 serving.

Note: We tested with Samuel Smith Oatmeal Stout.

Hot Fudge Sundae Shake

prep: 10 min.

A good hot fudge sundae brings out the child in us all. This version takes the sundae to a crazy-good level with brownie chunks and caramel topping. Microwave the caramel and fudge toppings according to package directions. Pick up brownies from your favorite local bakery.

1	pint vanilla bean ice cream		1	(8.5-ounce) can refrigerated instant whipped cream
½	cup milk		¼	cup crumbled brownies, divided
8	tablespoons hot fudge topping, warmed		4	maraschino cherries (with stems)
8	tablespoons caramel topping, warmed			

1. Process ice cream and milk in a blender until smooth, stopping to scrape down sides.
2. Divide half of ice-cream mixture among 4 (8-ounce) glasses. Top each with 1 tablespoon fudge topping and 1 tablespoon caramel topping. Repeat layers with remaining ice-cream mixture and fudge and caramel toppings.
3. Top each with instant whipped cream; sprinkle each with 1 tablespoon crumbled brownies, and top with a cherry. Serve immediately. **Yield:** 4 servings.

Note: We tested with Häagen-Dazs Vanilla Bean Ice Cream and Smucker's Hot Fudge and Caramel-Flavored Toppings.

Birthday Cake with Milk Chocolate
Frosting, page 343

food for friends

Sour Cream Cornbread

Sour Cream Cornbread

prep: 8 min. • bake: 27 min.

1½ cups self-rising white cornmeal mix
½ cup all-purpose flour
1 (14.75-ounce) can low-sodium cream-style corn
1 (8-ounce) container light sour cream

3 large eggs, lightly beaten
2 tablespoons chopped fresh cilantro
½ cup (2 ounces) 2% reduced-fat shredded Cheddar cheese (optional)

1. Preheat oven to 450°. Heat a 10-inch cast-iron skillet in oven 5 minutes.
2. Stir together cornmeal mix and flour in a large bowl; add corn and next 3 ingredients, stirring just until blended. Pour batter into hot lightly greased skillet. Top with cheese, if desired.
3. Bake at 450° for 22 to 24 minutes or until golden brown and cornbread pulls away from sides of skillet. **Yield:** 8 servings.

Hot-Water Cornbread

prep: 5 min. • cook: 6 min. per batch

2 cups white cornmeal
¼ teaspoon baking powder
1¼ teaspoons salt
1 teaspoon sugar
¼ cup half-and-half

1 tablespoon vegetable oil
1 to 2 cups boiling water
Vegetable oil
Softened butter

1. Combine first 4 ingredients in a bowl; stir in half-and-half and 1 tablespoon oil. Gradually add boiling water, stirring until batter is the consistency of grits.
2. Pour oil to a depth of ½ inch into a large heavy skillet; place over medium-high heat. Scoop batter into a ¼ cup measure; drop into hot oil, and fry, in batches, 3 minutes on each side or until golden. Drain on paper towels. Serve with softened butter. **Yield:** 1 dozen.

Note: The amount of boiling water needed varies depending on the type of cornmeal used. Stone-ground (coarsely ground) cornmeal requires more liquid.

Hearty Black-eyed Peas

Hearty Black-eyed Peas

prep: 10 min. • cook: 1 hr., 35 min.

Serve these slow-simmered peas plain or with rice and cornbread.

3 cups low-sodium chicken broth	4 whole jalapeño peppers (optional)
1 medium onion, chopped	1 (16-ounce) package dried black-eyed
1 smoked ham hock	peas
1 bay leaf	1 teaspoon salt
½ teaspoon pepper	

1. Bring 3 cups water, broth, next 4 ingredients, and, if desired, jalapeños to a boil in a Dutch oven; cover, reduce heat, and simmer 30 minutes.

2. Rinse and sort peas according to package directions. Add peas and ½ teaspoon salt to Dutch oven, and cook, covered, 1 hour or until peas are tender. If desired, remove meat from ham hock, finely chop, and return to Dutch oven. Season with remaining ½ teaspoon salt or to taste. Remove and discard bay leaf. **Yield:** 4 to 6 servings.

Quick Hoppin' John

prep: 10 min. • cook: 10 min. • stand: 5 min.

This peas-and-rice dish is the ideal accompaniment with pork or ham— and not just on New Year's Day but year-round.

3 bacon slices, chopped	1 cup quick long-grain rice, uncooked
½ cup chopped celery	2 tablespoons chopped fresh parsley
⅓ cup chopped onion	½ teaspoon dried thyme
1 (15-ounce) can black-eyed peas, undrained	

1. Cook bacon in a large saucepan until crisp, stirring often. Add celery and onion; cook, stirring constantly, until vegetables are tender.

2. Stir in 1 cup water and peas; bring to a boil. Cover, reduce heat, and simmer 5 minutes. Stir in rice, parsley, and thyme. Remove from heat; cover and let stand 5 minutes or until liquid is absorbed and rice is tender. **Yield:** 2 to 4 servings.

Holiday Ham

prep: 25 min. • bake: 2 hr.

Baked ham is great to have on hand during the holidays. Use it to make Ham-and-Dijon Biscuits (page 340), or serve it for breakfast along with hot biscuits, cheese grits, and fresh fruit.

make ahead

1 (8- to 10-pound) fully cooked, bone-in ham
1 (0.62-ounce) jar whole cloves
1 (16-ounce) package dark brown sugar
1 cup spicy brown mustard

1 cup apple cider
½ cup bourbon
1 cup hot brewed coffee (optional)
Garnishes: fresh rosemary, fresh sage, orange wedges

1. Preheat oven to 350°. Remove skin from ham, and trim fat to ¼-inch thickness. Make shallow cuts in fat in a diamond pattern. Push cloves into ham in a decorative pattern; place ham in a lightly greased roasting pan or 13- x 9-inch pan.

2. Stir together brown sugar and next 3 ingredients. Pour mixture over ham.

3. Bake at 350° on lower oven rack for 2 to 2½ hours or until a meat thermometer inserted into thickest portion registers 140°, basting with pan juices every 20 minutes. Shield ham after 1½ hours to prevent excessive browning, if necessary. Remove ham to a serving platter, and let cool.

4. Meanwhile, if desired, stir coffee into drippings to loosen browned particles in pan. Pour drippings into a saucepan, and cook 5 to 8 minutes or until slightly thickened. Serve sauce with ham. Garnish ham platter, if desired. Cover and store ham and sauce separately in refrigerator for up to 5 days. **Yield:** 12 servings.

Tomato Aspic

prep: 30 min. • cook: 5 min. • chill: 3 hr., 30 min.

Tomato aspic is known as the perfect fare for a ladies' luncheon or a festive spring brunch.

3	envelopes unflavored gelatin
4	cups tomato juice, divided
1	tablespoon refrigerated horseradish
2	teaspoons Worcestershire sauce
1	teaspoon hot sauce
½	teaspoon celery salt

⅔ cup finely chopped green bell pepper
⅔ cup finely chopped celery
1 tablespoon plus 1 teaspoon grated onion
1 medium cucumber
Curly leaf lettuce

1. Sprinkle gelatin over 1 cup tomato juice in a medium saucepan; let stand 1 minute. Cook over medium heat, stirring constantly, 3 to 5 minutes or until gelatin dissolves. Remove from heat; transfer mixture to a large bowl.

2. Stir in remaining 3 cups tomato juice, horseradish, and next 3 ingredients. Chill mixture to the consistency of unbeaten egg whites. Fold in bell pepper, celery, and onion. Spoon tomato mixture into 8 lightly oiled individual ½-cup molds. Cover and chill at least 3 hours or until firm.

3. Score cucumber with a fork. Thinly slice cucumber. Place lettuce leaves on individual salad plates or on 2 large pedestals, and arrange cucumber slices in a circle over lettuce leaves.

4. Unmold salads onto prepared plates or pedestals. **Yield:** 8 servings.

"This dish is a **favored** side dish or first course throughout the South. Check your grandmother's cabinets for vintage aspic molds."

Sally's Cheese Straws

Sally's Cheese Straws

prep: 15 min. • cook: 8 min. per batch

1 (16-ounce) block sharp Cheddar cheese, shredded (not preshredded), at room temperature	¼ cup butter, softened
	1 teaspoon salt
	¼ teaspoon ground red pepper
1½ cups all-purpose flour	⅛ teaspoon dry mustard

1. Process all ingredients in a food processor about 30 seconds or until mixture forms a ball.
2. Preheat oven to 375°. Fit a cookie press with a bar-shaped disk, and shape dough into straws, following manufacturer's instructions, on ungreased baking sheets. Cut ribbons crosswise with a knife to make individual straws.
3. Bake at 375° for 8 to 10 minutes or until lightly browned. Transfer to wire racks to cool.
Yield: about 8 dozen.

Curried Chicken Salad Tea Sandwiches

prep: 1 hr.

Tea sandwiches like these (as well as ham biscuits) display beautifully on tiered plates topped with a small bouquet of flowers for a wedding day menu (see page 340 for inspiration).

4 cups finely chopped cooked chicken	1 (2¼-ounce) package slivered almonds, toasted
3 (8-ounce) packages cream cheese, softened	1 tablespoon curry powder
¾ cup dried cranberries, chopped	1 tablespoon freshly grated ginger
½ cup sweetened flaked coconut, toasted	½ teaspoon salt
6 green onions, minced	½ teaspoon pepper
2 celery ribs, diced	48 whole-grain bread slices

1. Stir together first 11 ingredients. Spread mixture on 1 side each of 24 bread slices; top with remaining 24 bread slices. Trim crusts from sandwiches; cut each sandwich into 4 rectangles with a serrated knife. **Yield:** about 25 servings.

Ham-and-Dijon Biscuits With Caramelized Onion Butter

prep: 17 min. • bake: 13 min. per batch

These Southern ham biscuits certainly qualify as wedding reception worthy, but they're equally at home on a holiday sideboard. We recommend using Holiday Ham (page 334) for this recipe. You can also use any baked ham or even thinly sliced ham from the deli.

freezable • make ahead

9	cups all-purpose baking mix	¼	cup honey
2	cups milk		Caramelized Onion Butter
½	cup Dijon mustard		Ham (about 2 pounds)

1. Preheat oven to 450°. Make a well in center of baking mix in a large bowl.

2. Whisk together milk, mustard, and honey. Add milk mixture to baking mix, stirring just until moistened.

3. Turn out soft dough onto a floured surface; knead 3 or 4 times.

4. Roll half of dough at a time to ½-inch thickness; cut with a 2-inch round cutter, and place on lightly greased baking sheets. Reroll dough, and cut scraps.

5. Bake at 450° for 8 minutes or until lightly browned. Split warm biscuits. Spread with Caramelized Onion Butter, and fill with slivers of ham. Cover biscuits loosely with aluminum foil.

6. Reduce oven temperature to 350°. Bake at 350° for 5 to 7 minutes or just until thoroughly heated. **Yield:** 4 dozen.

Note: To make ahead, place assembled biscuits in an airtight container, and chill up to 8 hours, or freeze up to 3 weeks. Thaw frozen biscuits in refrigerator. To reheat, place biscuits on baking sheets, and cover loosely with aluminum foil. Bake at 350° for 10 to 12 minutes or until heated.

Caramelized Onion Butter

prep: 5 min. • cook: 15 min.

1¾	cups butter, softened	¼	cup firmly packed brown sugar
2	large sweet onions, finely chopped	1	tablespoon balsamic vinegar

1. Melt ¼ cup butter over medium-high heat in a large skillet. Add onions and brown sugar, and cook, stirring often, 15 to 20 minutes or until a deep caramel color. Remove from heat; cool slightly. Stir in remaining 1½ cups butter and vinegar. Use in recipe above, or cover and chill. Return to room temperature before serving. **Yield:** 2½ cups.

Birthday Cake

prep: 15 min. • bake: 25 min. • cool: 25 min. • freeze: 4 hr. • stand: 2 hr.

This recipe bakes up into a tender three-layer white cake. (Freezing the layers before frosting them makes assembly easy.) It's an ideal birthday cake for young ones.

make ahead

½ cup butter, softened	⅔ cup milk
½ cup shortening	2 teaspoons vanilla extract
2 cups sugar	¾ teaspoon almond extract
3 cups cake flour	6 egg whites
4 teaspoons baking powder	Milk Chocolate Frosting
½ teaspoon salt	Garnish: multicolored candy sprinkles

1. Preheat oven to 325°. Beat butter and shortening at medium speed with an electric mixer until creamy; gradually add sugar, beating well.

2. Combine flour, baking powder, and salt; add to butter mixture alternately with milk and ⅔ cup water, beginning and ending with flour mixture. Beat at low speed until blended after each addition. Stir in extracts.

3. Beat egg whites at high speed with electric mixer until stiff peaks form; fold about one-third of egg whites into batter. Gradually fold in remaining egg whites. Pour cake batter into 3 greased and floured 8-inch round cake pans.

4. Bake at 325° for 25 to 30 minutes or until a wooden pick inserted in center comes out clean. Cool in pans on wire racks 10 minutes. Remove from pans to wire racks, and let cool 15 minutes. Wrap each layer in plastic wrap. Freeze 4 hours.

5. Unwrap frozen cake layers. Spread Milk Chocolate Frosting between layers and on top and sides of cake. Let stand at room temperature 2 hours before serving. Garnish, if desired. **Yield:** 12 servings.

Milk Chocolate Frosting

prep: 10 min.

1 cup butter, softened	⅓ cup unsweetened cocoa
6 cups powdered sugar	½ cup milk

1. Beat butter at medium speed with an electric mixer until creamy. Add remaining ingredients, beating until smooth. **Yield:** 4 cups.

Homemade Limeade

Homemade Limeade

prep: 20 min. • chill: 8 hr.

For a fun garnish, thread lime slices onto wooden skewers and float the skewers in the pitcher or in tall glasses.

1½	cups sugar		1½	cups fresh lime juice (10 to 14 limes)
½	cup boiling water		5	cups cold water
2	teaspoons lime zest			Garnishes: lime slices, fresh mint sprigs

1. Stir together sugar and boiling water until sugar dissolves.
2. Stir in lime zest, lime juice, and cold water. Chill 8 hours. Garnish, if desired. **Yield:** 8 cups.

Variation

Homemade Lemonade: Substitute lemon zest and lemon juice for lime zest and lime juice.

make ahead • portable

Lemonade Iced Tea

prep: 10 min. • cook: 5 min. • steep: 10 min.

3	cups water		4	cups cold water
2	family-size tea bags		1	(6-ounce) can frozen lemonade
1	(1-ounce) package fresh mint leaves			concentrate, thawed
	(about 1 cup loosely packed)			Garnish: fresh citrus slices
½	cup sugar			

1. Bring 3 cups water to a boil in a 2-quart saucepan. Remove from heat, add tea bags, and stir in fresh mint. Cover and steep 10 minutes.
2. Remove and discard tea bags and mint. Stir in sugar until dissolved.
3. Pour tea into a 3-quart container, and stir in 4 cups cold water and lemonade concentrate. Serve over ice. Garnish, if desired. **Yield:** 8 cups.

Variations

• **Bourbon-Lemonade Iced Tea:** Prepare recipe as directed, and stir in 1 cup bourbon. **Yield:** 9 cups.
• **Spiced Dark Rum-Lemonade Iced Tea:** Prepare recipe as directed, and stir in 1 cup spiced dark rum. **Yield:** 9 cups.

Patriotic Cupcakes

prep: 40 min. • bake: 18 min. • cool: 55 min.

Spreading frosting on cupcakes can be time-consuming. You'll love our quick-and-easy technique using a zip-top plastic freezer bag.

make ahead

2 cups sugar	½ teaspoon baking soda
1 cup butter, softened	1 cup buttermilk
2 large eggs	24 paper baking cups
2 teaspoons fresh lemon juice	5-Cup Cream Cheese Frosting (page 287)
1 teaspoon vanilla extract	24 miniature American flags
2½ cups cake flour	

1. Preheat oven to 350°. Beat sugar and butter at medium speed with an electric mixer until creamy. Add eggs, 1 at a time, beating until yellow disappears after each addition. Beat in lemon juice and vanilla.

2. Combine flour and baking soda in a small bowl; add to sugar mixture alternately with buttermilk, beginning and ending with flour mixture. Beat at medium speed just until blended after each addition.

3. Place 24 paper baking cups in 2 (12-cup) muffin pans. Spoon batter into baking cups, filling two-thirds full.

4. Bake at 350° for 18 to 22 minutes or until a wooden pick inserted in center comes out clean. Cool in pans on a wire rack 10 minutes. Remove cupcakes from pans to wire rack, and cool 45 minutes or until completely cool.

5. Spoon 5-Cup Cream Cheese Frosting into a zip-top plastic freezer bag (do not seal). Snip 1 corner of bag to make a hole (about 1 inch in diameter). Pipe frosting in little loops onto tops of cupcakes as desired. Insert 1 flag into top of each cupcake. **Yield:** 2 dozen.

Note: To make ahead, bake and cool cupcakes as directed. Do not frost and decorate. Double-wrap cupcakes in plastic wrap and heavy-duty aluminum foil, or place in airtight containers, and freeze up to 1 month.

Roast Turkey and Gravy

prep: 14 min. • bake: 2 hr., 20 min. • cook: 5 min. • stand: 15 min.

1	(12- to 14-pound) turkey	2	large carrots, cut into 3-inch pieces
1	tablespoon salt	3	celery ribs with leaves, cut into 3-inch
2	teaspoons pepper		pieces
½	cup butter, softened	4	cups hot water
1	Golden Delicious apple, quartered	⅓	cup all-purpose flour
1	large yellow onion, quartered		Cornbread Dressing (page 351)

1. Preheat oven to 425°. Remove giblets and neck from turkey. Rinse turkey; reserve giblets and neck for another use.

2. Rinse turkey with cold water, and pat dry. Sprinkle cavity with ½ tablespoon salt and 1 teaspoon pepper. Rub skin of turkey with butter, and sprinkle with remaining ½ tablespoon salt and 1 teaspoon pepper.

3. Place apple, onion, carrot, and celery in turkey cavity. Lift wing tips up and over back, and tuck under bird. Place turkey, breast side up, on a lightly greased rack in a roasting pan.

4. Bake at 425° on lower oven rack 20 minutes. Reduce oven temperature to 325°. Add hot water to pan, and bake 2 to 2½ hours or until a meat thermometer inserted in turkey thigh registers 170°, shielding turkey with foil after 1 hour and basting with pan juices every 20 minutes. Let stand 15 minutes. Transfer to a serving platter; reserve 2½ cups drippings.

5. Whisk together drippings and ⅓ cup flour in a medium saucepan. Cook over medium heat, whisking constantly, 5 to 7 minutes or until thick and bubbly. Season gravy to taste. **Yield:** 12 to 14 servings.

"The secrets to a **juicy and succulent** turkey are, first, to select a fresh, free-range bird and, secondly, not to overcook it."

Classic Sweet Potato Casserole

Cornbread Dressing

prep: 15 min. • bake: 1 hr., 5 min.

make ahead

1	cup butter, divided	3	cups soft breadcrumbs
3	cups white cornmeal	3	cups finely chopped celery
1	cup all-purpose flour	2	cups finely chopped onion
2	tablespoons sugar	½	cup finely chopped fresh sage or
2	teaspoons baking powder		1 tablespoon dried rubbed sage
1½	teaspoons salt	5	(10½-ounce) cans condensed chicken
1	teaspoon baking soda		broth, undiluted
7	large eggs	1	tablespoon freshly ground pepper
3	cups buttermilk		

1. Preheat oven to 425°. Place ½ cup butter in a 13- x 9-inch pan; heat in oven at 425° for 4 minutes. Combine cornmeal and next 5 ingredients; whisk in 3 eggs and buttermilk.
2. Pour butter from pan into batter, stirring until blended. Pour batter into pan. Bake at 425° for 30 minutes or until golden. Cool. Crumble cornbread into a bowl; stir in breadcrumbs; set aside.
3. Melt remaining ½ cup butter in a large skillet over medium heat; add celery and onion, and sauté until tender. Stir in sage, and sauté 1 more minute.
4. Stir vegetables, remaining 4 eggs, chicken broth, and pepper into cornbread mixture; spoon into 1 lightly greased 13- x 9-inch baking dish and 1 lightly greased 8-inch square baking dish. Cover and chill 8 hours, if desired. Preheat oven to 375°. Bake dressing, uncovered, at 375° for 35 to 40 minutes or until golden brown. **Yield:** 16 to 18 servings.

Classic Sweet Potato Casserole

prep: 20 min. • bake: 1 hr., 40 min. • cool: 20 min. • stand: 20 min.

4½	pounds sweet potatoes	¼	teaspoon salt
1	cup granulated sugar	1¼	cups cornflakes cereal, crushed
½	cup butter, softened	¼	cup chopped pecans
¼	cup milk	1	tablespoon brown sugar
2	large eggs	1	tablespoon butter, melted
1	teaspoon vanilla extract	1½	cups miniature marshmallows

1. Preheat oven to 400°. Bake sweet potatoes at 400° for 1 hour or until tender. Let stand until cool to touch (about 20 minutes); peel and mash sweet potatoes. Reduce oven temperature to 350°.
2. Beat sweet potatoes, granulated sugar, and next 5 ingredients at medium speed with an electric mixer until smooth. Spoon into a greased 11- x 7-inch baking dish. Combine cornflakes cereal and next 3 ingredients in a bowl. Sprinkle over casserole in diagonal rows 2 inches apart.
3. Bake at 350° for 30 minutes. Remove from oven; let stand 10 minutes. Sprinkle marshmallows in alternate rows between cornflake mixture; bake 10 minutes. Let stand 10 minutes before serving. **Yield:** 6 to 8 servings.

Fresh Cranberry Congealed Salad

prep: 30 min. • chill: 8 hr., 30 min.

make ahead

1	(12-ounce) package fresh cranberries
½	cup sugar
3	(3-ounce) packages raspberry-flavored gelatin
2	cups boiling water
2	cups cranberry juice, chilled
1	(8-ounce) can crushed pineapple, undrained
2	celery ribs, diced (1 cup)
⅔	cup chopped pecans, toasted
	Lettuce leaves
	Garnishes: fresh cranberries, fresh mint sprigs

1. Process cranberries in a food processor 30 seconds or until coarsely chopped, stopping once to scrape down sides.

2. Stir together cranberries and sugar in a bowl; set aside.

3. Stir together gelatin and boiling water in a large bowl 2 minutes or until gelatin dissolves. Add juice, and chill 30 minutes or until consistency of unbeaten egg whites.

4. Stir in cranberry mixture, pineapple, celery, and pecans. Spoon mixture into a lightly greased 10-cup Bundt pan; cover and chill 8 hours or until firm.

5. Unmold salad onto a lettuce-lined platter. Garnish, if desired. **Yield:** 12 servings.

> This festive salad adds **color** to your table, as well as a sweet-tart flavor.

Refrigerator Yeast Rolls

prep: 18 min. • chill: 8 hr. • rise: 45 min. • bake: 14 min.

You may know these as Parker House rolls, but whatever the name, they are classic buttery, soft, folded dinner rolls for any night of the week.

make ahead

1	(¼-ounce) envelope active dry yeast
2	cups warm water (100° to 110°)
6	cups bread flour
½	cup sugar

2	teaspoons salt
½	cup shortening
2	large eggs, lightly beaten
½	cup butter, melted

1. Stir together yeast and warm water in a medium bowl; let stand 5 minutes.

2. Stir together flour, sugar, and salt in a large bowl.

3. Cut shortening into flour mixture with a pastry blender until crumbly; stir in yeast mixture and eggs just until blended. (Do not overmix.) Cover and chill 8 hours.

4. Roll dough to ¼-inch thickness on a well-floured surface (dough will be soft); cut with a 2½-inch round cutter.

5. Brush rounds with melted butter. Make a crease across each round with the dull edge of a knife, and fold in half; gently press edges to seal. Place rolls in a greased 15- x 10-inch jelly-roll pan with sides touching or in 2 (9-inch) square pans. Cover and let rise in a warm place (85°), free from drafts, 45 minutes or until doubled in bulk.

6. Prehcat oven to 400°. Bake at 400° for 14 minutes or until golden. **Yield:** about 3 dozen.

If you have any leftovers of these **melt-in-your-mouth** treats, serve them with ham for tasty little sandwiches.

Pumpkin Chess Pie

prep: 15 min. • bake: 1 hr., 10 min. • chill: 8 hr.

Pumpkin pie is traditionally served around the holidays, but this version with its luscious sauce is so good you'll want to serve it year-round.

½ (14.1-ounce) package refrigerated piecrusts
1 (15-ounce) can unsweetened pumpkin
2 cups sugar
½ cup butter, softened
3 large eggs
½ cup half-and-half

1½ teaspoons vanilla extract
¾ teaspoon salt
½ teaspoon ground cinnamon
¼ teaspoon ground ginger
¼ teaspoon ground cloves
Praline Sauce

1. Preheat oven to 350°. Fit piecrust in a 9-inch pie plate according to package directions; fold edges under, and crimp.

2. Beat pumpkin, sugar, and butter in a large bowl at medium speed with an electric mixer until smooth. Add eggs and next 6 ingredients, beating until blended. Pour filling into prepared crust.

3. Bake at 350° for 1 hour and 10 minutes or until almost set. Cool pie completely on a wire rack. Chill for 8 hours. Serve with Praline Sauce. **Yield:** 8 servings.

Praline Sauce

prep: 5 min. • cook: 1 min.

This rich sauce is also good spooned over ice cream and makes a perfect holiday gift.

1 cup firmly packed brown sugar
½ cup half-and-half
½ cup butter

½ cup chopped pecans, toasted
½ teaspoon vanilla extract

1. Combine first 3 ingredients in a small saucepan over medium heat. Bring to a boil; cook, stirring constantly, 1 minute. Remove from heat; stir in pecans and vanilla. Cool completely. **Yield:** about 2 cups.

Roasted Pecan Fudge

prep: 15 min. • soak: 20 min. • stand: 1 hr., 30 min.

Pair this creamy, rich chocolate fudge with Peanut Butter Fudge (recipe follows) in a tin for gift giving.

2½	cups pecan halves	2	tablespoons butter
4	tablespoons salt	2	cups miniature marshmallows
1⅔	cups sugar	1½	cups semisweet chocolate morsels
⅔	cup evaporated milk	2	teaspoons vanilla extract

1. Preheat oven to 450°. Soak pecan halves in water to cover 20 minutes; drain well. Sprinkle 2 tablespoons salt over bottom of a 15- x 10-inch jelly-roll pan. Arrange pecans in a single layer in pan; sprinkle with 2 more tablespoons salt. Place pecans in hot oven, and turn off oven. Let stand in oven 1 hour and 30 minutes. Toss pecans in a strainer to remove excess salt. Coarsely chop pecans, and cool.

2. Bring sugar, evaporated milk, and butter to a boil in a large heavy saucepan over medium heat; boil, stirring constantly, until a candy thermometer registers 234° (soft-ball stage) about 7 minutes.

3. Remove from heat; stir in marshmallows and chocolate morsels until smooth. Stir in 2 teaspoons vanilla and chopped pecans.

4. Pour fudge into a buttered 8-inch square pan, and cool completely. Cut into squares. **Yield:** 5 dozen pieces.

Test Kitchen Tip

Soft-ball stage (234°) is a candy-making term. Drop a small amount of boiling mixture (in this recipe, the sugar, milk, and butter combination) into a glass cup of cold water. When it forms a soft ball that flattens as you remove it from the water, you've reached the soft-ball stage.

Peanut Butter Fudge

prep: 10 min. • cook: 10 min. • cool: 1 hr.

1	(5-ounce) can evaporated milk	1	(10-ounce) package peanut butter morsels
1⅔	cups sugar	1	teaspoon vanilla extract
½	teaspoon salt	½	cup chopped peanuts
1¾	cups miniature marshmallows		

1. Bring first 3 ingredients to a boil in a large saucepan over medium-high heat. Reduce heat to medium, and cook, stirring constantly, 5 minutes; remove from heat. Add marshmallows, peanut butter morsels, and vanilla; stir until smooth. Pour fudge into a greased 8-inch square pan. Gently press peanuts into top of warm fudge. Let cool 1 hour or until completely cool. Cut into squares. **Yield:** 3 dozen pieces.

Metric Equivalents

The recipes that appear in this cookbook use the standard U.S. method for measuring liquid and dry or solid ingredients (teaspoons, tablespoons, and cups). The information in the following charts is provided to help cooks outside the United States successfully use these recipes. All equivalents are approximate.

Metric Equivalents for Different Types of Ingredients

A standard cup measure of a dry or solid ingredient will vary in weight depending on the type of ingredient. A standard cup of liquid is the same volume for any type of liquid. Use the following chart when converting standard cup measures to grams (weight) or milliliters (volume).

Standard Cup	Fine Powder (ex. flour)	Grain (ex. rice)	Granular (ex. sugar)	Liquid Solids (ex. butter)	Liquid (ex. milk)
1	140 g	150 g	190 g	200 g	240 ml
¾	105 g	113 g	143 g	150 g	180 ml
⅔	93 g	100 g	125 g	133 g	160 ml
½	70 g	75 g	95 g	100 g	120 ml
⅓	47 g	50 g	63 g	67 g	80 ml
¼	35 g	38 g	48 g	50 g	60 ml
⅛	18 g	19 g	24 g	25 g	30 ml

Useful Equivalents for Dry Ingredients by Weight
(To convert ounces to grams, multiply the number of ounces by 30.)

1 oz	=	1/16 lb	=	30 g
4 oz	=	¼ lb	=	120 g
8 oz	=	½ lb	=	240 g
12 oz	=	¾ lb	=	360 g
16 oz	=	1 lb	=	480 g

Useful Equivalents for Length
(To convert inches to centimeters, multiply the number of inches by 2.5.)

1 in			=	2.5 cm		
6 in	=	½ ft	=	15 cm		
12 in	=	1 ft	=	30 cm		
36 in	=	3 ft	= 1 yd	=	90 cm	
40 in			=	100 cm	=	1 m

Useful Equivalents for Liquid Ingredients by Volume

¼ tsp					=	1 ml
½ tsp					=	2 ml
1 tsp					=	5 ml
3 tsp	=	1 Tbsp		=	½ fl oz	=	15 ml
		2 Tbsp	=	⅛ cup	=	1 fl oz	=	30 ml
		4 Tbsp	=	¼ cup	=	2 fl oz	=	60 ml
		5⅓ Tbsp	=	⅓ cup	=	3 fl oz	=	80 ml
		8 Tbsp	=	½ cup	=	4 fl oz	=	120 ml
		10⅔ Tbsp	=	⅔ cup	=	5 fl oz	=	160 ml
		12 Tbsp	=	¾ cup	=	6 fl oz	=	180 ml
		16 Tbsp	=	1 cup	=	8 fl oz	=	240 ml
		1 pt	=	2 cups	=	16 fl oz	=	480 ml
		1 qt	=	4 cups	=	32 fl oz	=	960 ml
					33 fl oz	–	1000 ml

Useful Equivalents for Cooking/Oven Temperatures

	Fahrenheit	Celsius	Gas Mark
Freeze water	32° F	0° C	
Room temperature	68° F	20° C	
Boil water	212° F	100° C	
Bake	325° F	160° C	3
	350° F	180° C	4
	375° F	190° C	5
	400° F	200° C	6
	425° F	220° C	7
	450° F	230° C	8
Broil			Grill

Index